THE

The Lord's Prayer

The Greatest Prayer in the World

Peter Lewis

Hodder & Stoughton
LONDON SYDNEY AUCKLAND

For my mother, Winifred Lewis of Nantyglo,
who first taught me to pray

Biblical quotations are taken from the New International
Version

Copyright © Peter Lewis 1995

First published in Great Britain in 1995 by
Hodder and Stoughton, a division of Hodder Headline PLC

British Library Cataloguing in Publication Data
A record for this book is available from the British Library

ISBN 0 340 62143 5

Typeset by Hewer Text Composition Services, Edinburgh
Printed and bound in Great Britain by
Cox & Wyman Ltd, Reading, Berks.

Hodder and Stoughton Ltd,
A division of Hodder Headline PLC
338 Euston Road
London NW1 3BH

CONTENTS

Part Three: Give us today our daily bread

Part Four: Forgive us our debts as we also have forgiven our debtors

Part Five: And lead us not into temptation, but deliver us from the evil one

Part Six: For yours is the kingdom and the power and the glory for ever. Amen

PREFACE

The cover of this book features a skyscraper. And prayer too is a kind of skyscraper. It quite literally reaches beyond the skies – and gets there! It rises above the landscape while still being firmly grounded in it. It helps us to see the scene from a different perspective and enables us to respond to the needs around us with more perception and wisdom and effectiveness than we would otherwise have. Like the skyscape of a modern city, prayer in today's world is an engaged relevance, not an engaging irrelevance. This is a book a great prayer about and the truths which are the firm foundation of all prayer. It is not about prayer in general, nor is reading it praying! Yet it may be an elevator in the building of a prayer-life which will help the reader to gain new heights as he or she prays to our Father in heaven.

I would like in this preface to thank my publishers, Hodder and Stoughton, and in particular James Catford, who first welcomed the idea of such a book and encouraged it at every stage, and also my willing and indefatigable typist Mrs Barbara Walters, for doing the impossible – several times! As ever I record with gratitude and joy the love and support of my wife Valerie, whose prayer-life goes far in strengthening and sustaining me. Finally, and writing these words on the twenty-fifth anniversary of the beginning of my ministry here in Nottingham, I would like to record my love to and gratitude for the elders and members of the Cornerstone Church: 'The boundary lines have fallen for me in pleasant places; surely I have a delightful inheritance' (Psalm 16:6).

Peter Lewis
The Cornerstone Church
Nottingham
September 1994

INTRODUCTION – WHY PRAY?

It was a strange sight – a blind boy flying a kite with his father's help. A friend of the family watching dared to ask him a question, 'What do you get out of this when you can't see the kite'? The answer was simple enough, the boy replied, 'I can't see it but I can feel the pull.'

Christians might make a similar reply to the questions, 'Why pray to a God you can't see? Why put so much effort into an exercise so unquantifiable?' The answer might well be, 'I can't see what's happening but I can feel the pull.' It's true, I know, that often in the matter of a steady, faithful, disciplined prayer-life we think more in terms of 'push' than 'pull'! And so the question suggests itself, 'Why pray?'

The first and sufficient reason why we should pray is because God commands it God would not tell us to do a meaningless act. He puts meaning into life not futility. He would not tell us to do something which would waste our time and make a mockery of faith and obedience. If God tells us to pray then prayer has its value and point from him. His promise is its rationale and his power is its potential.

God repeatedly encourages us to pray, to honour his dominion, to seek his face, to discover his will and to enlist his help. He has made us for himself and prayer is an essential expression of that. We were made to pray. In prayer we assert the uniqueness of our humanity which is made to relate to God. We became a fallen race and futility entered our world[1] but prayer, believing prayer, prayer in response to the call of God, is a step away from futility towards fulfilment. Prayer always brings me a little closer to God, and whether I feel it so or not. If my prayer isn't answered, I am. Even if I do not feel anything has been achieved, God does.

Jesus says not 'If you pray' but 'When you pray'[2] and later, with characteristic understanding that 'the spirit is willing but the flesh is weak' tells his followers a parable 'to show them that they should always pray and not give up'.[3] Above all else in prayer they were to 'keep on asking . . . seeking . . . knocking'[4] the present continuous tense is repeatedly used for the Holy Spirit whose presence and power would characterise life in the kingdom of God.

Second, we should pray because God is glorified in it

Nothing glorifies God quite like prayer. No one shares the glory with Him in this. Prayer begins as it ends, recognising that His is 'the kingdom, the power and the glory'. Prayer gives God the glory of all his attributes or characteristics. It gives him the glory of his *omniscience* (the word means all knowing, all seeing) in addressing him. It gives him the glory of his *omnipotence* (all powerfulness) and his *goodness* in seeking his help. It gives him the glory of his *holiness* in making confession, of his *wisdom* in seeking guidance and of his *mercy, grace and love* in praise and thanksgiving. Nothing substitutes for prayer, it has its own unique part to play in honouring God.

Third, we should pray because people need our prayers

More things are wrought by prayer
Than this world dreams of. Wherefore let thy voice
Rise like a foundation for me night and day
For what are men better than sheep or goats
That nourish a blind life within the brain,
If knowing God they lift not hand of prayer
Both for themselves and those who call them friend?
For so the whole sound earth is every way
Bound by gold chains about the feet of God

Prayer is an activity of care, a sign of love when we take it upon ourselves to pray regularly for someone. It involves us in their life as a partner and friend. The self-contained life knows little of love but love opens us up to share other people's burdens and minister to others' needs; to become vulnerable, yes, but also to become an open channel for God through which he can pour his grace into needy lives.[5]

It is a striking fact that the apostle Paul who knew Christ's presence in his ministry with much unction and power, notwithstanding, pleads again and again for the prayers of his young churches:

> Pray also for me, that whenever I open my
> mouth, words may be given so that I will
> fearlessly make known the mystery of the
> gospel, for which I am an ambassador in
> chains. Pray that I may declare it
> fearlessly, as I should.[6]

If Paul needed prayer from people like ourselves in those early churches surely there are others that we know in ministry at home or abroad, sometimes in the hard places of the earth, with few securities and even fewer comforts who need the defence of our prayers,[7] the assistance of our prayers[8] and quite simply the love of our prayers.[9]

The fourth reason why we should pray is because we change as we pray As we pray we become more aware of God as central to everything, the key to everything and concerned about everything. This perception changes our attitude and approach in subtle ways. We become more dependent upon God, realising our weakness, our inadequacy and the danger of our own unchecked wisdom and wilfulness.[10] As we struggle with these things we become more conformed to God: to his nature, his will and his ways. Richard Foster in his *Celebration of Discipline* writes: 'To pray is to change. Prayer is the central avenue God uses to transform us.'

We may often struggle to pray, to submit to its disciplines, to respond to its calls; we may consquently feel we are no better after than before, no nearer our goals or God's. But that is just not true. The promises given to prayer were not given to extraordinary practitioners but to very ordinary believers. Prayer changes things and the first thing it changes is us! Though we do not see it we grow as we pray.

Fifth, we should pray because things change as we pray
Archbishop William Temple used to say, 'People tell me that answers to prayer are merely coincidences. I can only reply that when I pray coincidences happen and when I stop praying they stop happening.'

One of the most dramatic answers to prayer was given to a church I know in Dunstable. A series of brutal attacks and rapes were carried out in the area by a criminal who came to be known as 'The Fox' in the popular press becauses of his skill in evading the police. Eventually this local church held special prayer meetings for the capture of the criminal; they prayed specifically, forcefully, persistently. Soon after 'The Fox' was captured and a picture appeared in the papers of the criminal handcuffed between two policemen. Both policemen were members of that same praying church. Was that God's comment on 'coincidence'?

Notes

1 Ecc. 1:2.
2 Matt. 6:5–7, 9.
3 Luke 18:1.
4 Luke 11:9.
5 Gal. 6:2; Eph. 6:19, 20.
6 Eph. 6:19, 20.
7 Rom. 15:31.
8 Col. 4:3.
9 I Thess. 5:25, 26.
10 Prov. 3:5, 6.

I. OUR FATHER IN HEAVEN, HALLOWED BE YOUR NAME

1

OUR FATHER

The first two words of this prayer are a celebration: a celebration of God! We celebrate a relationship with him; a relationship which has in it the genius and glory of every other relationship: the pride of the parent, the security of the child, the confidence of friends, the pleasure of lovers and the joy of bride and groom. God has many names and titles to show his place in that relationship: King, Master, Shepherd, Friend etc. But 'Father' goes beyond them all and is the most profound of them all, indicating our ultimate identity and our supreme privilege, our dignity and our duty: 'How great is the love the Father has lavished on us, that we should be called children of God.'[1]

God is our *Father*; we belong to him. This one truth tells us who we are and why we are, it tells us how we must live and how we may die; it challenges us and it comforts us. It is now the first and most important truth about our relationship with God. We may not understand his essential being but we can understand his character and his relationship to us with its commitment, authority and love. He is not, after all, 'the unknown God': in Jesus Christ his Son he has become our Father-God.[2]

In the context of God I do not take this name or title in a gender-specific way. Take every characteristic of good parenthood, from father and mother, take every fond experience and valued association and raise it to the highest degree and you will have glimpsed the character of God, the Father and Mother of us all, the heavenly parent: strong and gentle, firm and tender, slow to anger, quick to forgive, encourage and embrace.

My first memory is of my mother's smile, her eyes shining with love and pleasure. I had done nothing to earn it (nor could I at two years old!), nor did I need to do

3

so. It was a love called by the old theologians *complacere* (literally 'complacent', but in the original sense of 'resting on' with delight); that is, a love that simply delighted in its object. That is principally the love with which the Father loves the Son, but the wonder of grace is this gospel: in that when we are 'in Christ' we ourselves become sharers of that love. Jesus revealed that in his prayer to his Father in John chapter 17: 'I have made you known to them, and will continue to make you known in order that the love you have for me may be in them.'[3]

It is often hard for us to think that God might love us in this simple, ungrudging, delighted way but in heaven and thereafter it will be evidently the case. Yet we are no less 'in Christ' now than then and while it is clear to us that we are unworthy and sinners still, who often grieve and even anger him, it is, alas, not so clear how it can be that in Christ he sees us with joy and satisfaction. The explanation lies in the crucial phrase 'in Christ', which recurs so often in the New Testament to describe the believer's standing before God, our place in the Father's plan and in the representative work of Christ.

Christ has become for us, 'wisdom from God – that is, our righteousness, holiness and redemption'.[4] Consequently, 'in him' we are complete: redeemed for God, forgiven by God and destined by God 'for the praise of his glory'.[5] So the love of God for us is one with the love the Father has for the Son[6] and on that secure love we can build better, stronger Christian lives.

My father as well as my mother helped me to understand the various facets of love. He was a man of immense integrity and real devotion, though less able to express his affections in words than my mother. He was a quiet, placid though strong-minded character with considerable gifts in music; a solid and reliable support to those who depended on him. He also embodied the saying that the best gift a father can ever give his children is to love their mother. Sadly without Christian faith himself, he yet inherited from a godly father an unshakeable sense of right and wrong. If ever I had robbed a bank and he came to know of it, he would have marched me to the prison cell in person. But he would also have visited me every day! Consequently my respect for my father was as great as my love; indeed to this day I regard respect as a quality of love (that is as giving quality to it) even if it is not exactly a condition of love. We sometimes have to go on loving even where we have lost respect for the loved one; but then, love, admirable as it may be, is weakened by the very object to which it goes out.

We hear too little of 'respect' these days, in or out of the home; and even in Christian circles 'reverence' is not an attitude much cultivated or perhaps even understood. When did you last hear or speak or even think of someone being 'God-fearing'? Yet the fear of God is a concept as biblical as the fatherhood of God. Of course the quality of this kind of 'fear' is not base or threatening, it is not terror or insecurity we are speaking of here, but reverence, respect, a recognition of his righteousness, truth and justice which will not compromise and which does not surrender its own character when it seeks to elevate ours.

Sometimes when I was in flight from my father the only safe place in the whole wide world was behind my mother's skirts. But where shall one go to escape the wrath of God? Only *to* God, whose mercies are more than our sins, whose love has honoured his justice once and for all, and who is always ready to forgive those who are truly sorry. No child rubbing their tear-stained face into their father's (as my children have done in years gone by) was ever more assured of complete forgiveness and every tender demonstration of acceptance and love, than the repentant believer turning from wrong-doing to their Father in heaven. No one delights in mercy more than 'the Father of compassion and the God of all comfort'.[7]

I realise, of course, that not everyone has good associations with the concept of a father. In our sinful, spoiled world of selfishness, cruelty and fractured relationships, even the father–child relationship has been betrayed and broken in many cases. And in a world of wars and sickness and sudden death many children have lost their birthright and been cheated of a parent. Yet in countless lives the earthly relationship has been in some small way the mirror of the divine.

He may be for you the Father you never had. You may have grown up with an aching gap in your life. But he knew: he drew you to himself, he led you to one who is the Son of God by nature that you might become a child of God by grace. He adopted you. By new birth you carry his name; 'born of the Spirit, washed in the blood' you have become 'partaker of the divine nature', for he dwells in you and will be with you and is shaping you in the beauty of holiness to make you like himself. You have a Father now – you are not cheated.

He may be for others a Father in stark contrast to their earthly parent. Perhaps it has been an effort for you to call him 'Father' because of past associations with an unworthy or unloving father. God stands in contrast to many earthly parents. They were brutal: he is gentle. They were indifferent: he is committed. They were foolish: he is wise. They were distant: he has no inhibitions. He is the Father you always wanted; and you are his wanted child. The knowledge of this lies at the heart of our peace and the celebration of this is the crowning glory of our prayers, said or sung.

Notes

1 1 John 3:1.
2 John 1:12.
3 John 17:26.
4 Rom. 1:17; 1 Cor. 1:30.
5 Eph. 1:4–12.
6 John 17:23.
7 2 Cor. 1:3.

2

OUR FATHER IN HEAVEN

In his book *Knowing God*, J.I. Packer warns us that Christians today largely lack a true appreciation of the majesty of God, adding: 'and that is one reason why our faith is so feeble and our worship so flabby. We are modern men and modern men though they cherish great thoughts of man have as a rule small thoughts of God.'[1]

One reason, perhaps, why the transcendence of God has less attraction for the contemporary mind, even of believers, is that in spite of our great thoughts about ourselves we feel increasingly lost in our ever-expanding universe and increasingly insignificant in our modern cities and in our technological society. We constantly need affirmation, attention, a place of our own in the scheme of things. So much of our modern world dwarfs us, towering over us like our skyscrapers and telling us we don't matter. In our village communities of the past we had identities, but in the modern industrial and technological world we have only an identity crisis, feeling anonymous and insecure. We are crushed by the greatness of what is created, we do not want to think too much of a power which towers even above that.

However we do not need to *oppose* God's greatness to our meaningfulness, for God himself has long ago brought them together and said: 'For this is what the high and lofty One says – he who lives for ever, whose name is holy: I live in a high and holy place, but also with him who is contrite and lowly in spirit, to receive the spirit of the lowly and to revive the heart of the contrite.'[2] And here our Lord Jesus himself tells us that the first and last, the supreme and the definitive truth about us is that we have a 'Father' who is 'in heaven'. And the more we consider those two things *together* the greater will be our joy and peace in believing.

For as we consider who he is we shall better know who *we* are:

> Praise, my soul, the King of heaven;
> To his feet thy tribute bring.
> Ransom'd, healed, restored, forgiven,
> Who like thee His praise should sing?[3]

In their book *Stephen Hawking: a life in science*, Michael White and John Gribben quote Hawking's conclusion from modern science's observation of the size of the physical universe around us: 'We are such insignificant creatures on a minor planet of a very average star in the outer suburbs of one of a hundred thousand million galaxies . . . that it is difficult to believe in a God that would care about us or even notice our existence.'[4] But this experience of our littleness and creation's vastness is not new at all. Three thousand years ago the Psalmist wrote of it – but with a very different conclusion. For the Psalmist might have known much less about creation than modern scientists but he knew far more about God!

> O Lord, our Lord
> how majestic is your name in all the earth!
> You have set your glory above the heavens . . .
> When I consider your heavens, the work of your
>   fingers,
> the moon and stars, which you have set in place,
> what is man that you are mindful of him,
> the son of man that you care for him?
> You made him a little lower than the heavenly beings
> and crowned him with glory and honour.[5]

The Psalmist knew that creation was big even if he didn't know just how big. He also knew that God was bigger,[6] so much so that size to him was irrelevant.[7] The God who was great in big things was even greater in small things – including his tender regard for us. And even in his knowledge of 'us' the Psalmist has something to

8

teach modern man and woman. For he knows we are not simply well-evolved animals or bits of nature but 'crowned with glory and honour', the glory and honour of being human, made in the image of our creator, and as such only 'a little lower than the heavenly beings'. He knew his God and therefore knew himself and his fellow human beings in a crucial respect; some modern scientists and anthropologists have yet to catch him up!

Notes

1 J.I. Packer, *Knowing God*, London, Hodder & Stoughton, 1977, p. 88.
2 Isa. 57:15.
3 'Praise, my soul, the King of Heaven', Henry Francis Lyte (1793–1847), based on Psalm 103.
4 Michael White and John Gribben, *Stephen Hawking: a life in science*, London, Penguin, 1992, p. 166.
5 Ps. 8:1, 3–5.
6 Cf. Isa. 40:12–14, 22, 26.
7 Cf. Isa. 40:10–11, 27–31.

3

THE GLORY OF OUR FATHER

The Bible is full of God's glory and majesty, his transcendence and his sovereignty, and so should be our awareness of him in prayer and praise. The heavenliness of God: his power and his majesty, his greatness and his glory were early lessons in the history of Israel, God's chosen people, and they are never lost or left behind in the ongoing biblical revelation concerning God. In the beginning he is there without beginning, the self-existent God,[1] the creator of the heavens and the earth. He is also distinct from his creation: in it yet above it, sustaining it yet transcending it; his creation cannot contain him.[2]

In a world of idolatry the spirituality of God was carefully guarded, yet at times God manifested himself on earth in a created glory, 'the glory of the Lord'. Even this was, properly speaking, indescribable. Moses, Aaron, the elders of Israel, having been ushered into the presence of the Lord could only speak of the splendour under his feet.[3] Moses alone was permitted to see God's 'back' but not his 'face', that is his retiring, not his full, glory.[4] Isaiah saw the fringe of God's glory, 'the hem of his robe' which filled the temple[5] and brought the young prophet to his knees in terror and self-revulsion. Ezekiel, who saw, perhaps, the most, could call what he saw only 'the appearance of the likeness of the glory of the Lord',[6] beautiful but fearful.

God's majesty is as moral as it is mighty; he is 'perfect in power, in love and purity', the righteous God who is 'the judge of all the earth'.[7] Where these things are most deeply felt, at the near approach of God to his people, there is a sense of *awe* which overcomes the best of them. At the burning bush Moses hid his face because he was afraid to look on God.[8] At the foot of Sinai the people said to Moses, 'Speak to us yourself and we will listen.

But do not have God speak to us or we will die.'[9] When Job at last felt God come near he said, 'I despise myself and repent in dust and ashes'[10], and young Isaiah cried out, 'I'm ruined, I'm unclean';[11] Ezekiel fell face down[12] and Daniel swooned and was drained of strength even to speak when God's angel, bearing but a reflected glory, approached him.[13] The glory of God shining from the face of the risen Christ, who is the image of the invisible God, blinded Saul of Tarsus[14] and when the apostle John saw it he records, 'I fell at his feet as though dead.'[15]

It is right that we should 'approach with confidence'[16] our Father in heaven when we pray. But it is also right that we should marvel at our privilege and even our safety in doing so! For the ancient Hebrew the Holy of Holies was a frightening place, and for the modern Christian it is only because Jesus has gone there as our redeemer and mediator that it has become our eternal home:[17]

> I stand before the Presence
> Of the Lord God of hosts,
> A child of my Father
> And an heir of his grace;
> For Jesus paid the debt for me,
> The veil was torn in two,
> And the Holy of Holies
> Has become my dwelling place.[18]

Notes

1 Gen. 1:1; Exod. 3:14.
2 1 Kgs. 8:27.
3 Exod. 24:10.
4 Exod. 33:23.
5 Isa. 6:1ff.
6 Ezek. 1:28.
7 Gen. 18:25.
8 Exod. 3:6.
9 Exod. 20:19.

10 Job 42:6.
11 Isa. 6:5.
12 Ezek. 1:28.
13 Dan. 10:8–9, 15–19.
14 Acts 9:3, 8.
15 Rev. 1:17.
16 Heb. 10:19.
17 Heb. chapters 9–10.
18 Mavis Ford, Springtide/Word Music (UK), 1980.

4

THE SOVEREIGNTY OF OUR FATHER

This God is God and there is no one beside him: 'I am the Lord, and there is no other.'[1] He is *eternal*, the aeons of creation are but passing moments to him: 'from everlasting to everlasting you are God.'[2] He is *omniscient*, seeing and knowing all that is, all that has been, and all that ever will be, planning and bringing to perfection all he has purposed.[3] No contradiction can finally defeat his plans for he is *omnipotent*, the Almighty God, who promises his people great and glorious things[4] – which sometimes seem unlikely or lost in a world of disappointments – but who says when faith is low, 'Is anything too hard for the Lord?'[5]

The doctrine of God's sovereignty is given not to crush us but to comfort us. We may sometimes have problems with the doctrine but we would have many more if he were not 'the sovereign Lord'! If he were only sovereign in heaven, what would be the point of praying this prayer on earth? If he were only sovereign in the Church, who would help us in the world? But in fact he is 'the sovereign Lord' the Most High of whom we can say, 'He is my refuge and my fortress, my God in whom I trust.'[6] Others have their 'contacts in high places' but we have a Father in the highest place of all: big enough for all our problems, concerned enough for all our cares, close enough to guide, protect and reassure. As we walk through life, problems meet us which dwarf us and we are tempted to feel hopeless as well as helpless. Yet when we kneel to pray in full recognition of God's greatness we see our problems themselves dwarfed before the God of all the earth, the sovereign and transcendent God – our Father.

When I was a boy I was frequently bullied, being an excitable but non-aggressive type of child; indeed I had little physical courage and went in daily dread of the village bullies at school and outside. Yet one day I walked through a gang of them without a qualm, smiling and nodding to one and another – and why? Only because *my father was with me*, strong enough and near enough to deal with any or all of them. Oddly his presence turned their contempt into something like friendliness as they nodded back and said polite enough hallos. So with the knowledge of our Father in heaven we can meet life's 'bullies', its fears, frustrations and failures, its sorrows and its losses, on new terms and with new resources. Indeed our Father in heaven can turn them to good, turning setbacks into stepping-stones, opponents into allies, losses into gains: 'And we know that in all things God works for the good of those who love him, who have been called according to his purpose.'[7]

Notes

1 Isa. 45:6.
2 Ps. 90:2.
3 Isa. 46:8–10.
4 Gen. 17:1; Jer. 29:11.
5 Gen. 18:14.
6 Ps. 91:2.
7 Rom. 8:28.

5

OUR HOLY FATHER

There is an extraordinary paradox in those two words 'Holy Father': they mean almost impossibly different things. The Hebrew word for 'holy' is *quadosh*, a word whose root probably means 'cut', and the essential idea is that God is 'cut off' from everything else; he is *different*, so different as to be immeasurably removed in his essential being from all other things. They are created; he is uncreated. They are finite; he is infinite. They are (now) spoiled by sin; he is 'too pure to look on evil' or to 'tolerate wrong'.[1] Even unfallen angels bow in awe before the eternal mystery of God's 'otherness' and the brightest and the best of his human children are, like the young Isaiah, staggered and threatened by his aweful purity.[2]

But if 'holy' means 'other', 'Father' means 'like'; it carries overtones of similarity, of belonging, of identity. It was perhaps because Israel had to learn the lesson of Yahweh's holiness that it hesitated to call him 'Father', certainly in the intimate sense of Jesus' Aramaic 'Abba'. Father to the nation he might be called[3] but to domesticate or even personalise such a relationship in that way must have seemed shocking and presumptuous. But then Jesus came . . .

Donald Guthrie in his *New Testament theology* writes: 'It is the idea of the Fatherhood of God which is most characteristic of New Testament teaching and especially of the teaching of Jesus.'[4] The meaning and implication of that fatherhood is strikingly brought out in Jesus's use of 'Abba' when addressing God. This was the domestic and confident form of the name used by all Jewish children at home for their earthly fathers, and one which was used thereafter by Jesus's earliest followers for their Father in heaven.[5] 'The Abba form', says Guthrie, 'conveys a sense

15

of intimacy and familiarity which introduced an entirely new factor into man's approach to God.'[6]

This does not at all mean that God is less majestic, less exalted, less awesome than had been thought. It is not meant to lower God but to lift up ourselves. It is not that *God* is diminished, only that *we* are exalted. He is still 'fearful in praises' but we are called to enter, with complete safety and confidence, that daunting glory which awes angels and would have destroyed sinners.

The writer to the Hebrews perfectly unites the reverence due to God with the confidence proper to sons and daughters when, in view of the whole priestly work of Jesus Christ, he urges his readers: 'Let us then approach the throne of grace with confidence, so that we may receive mercy and find grace to help us in our time of need'[7] and later:

> Therefore, brothers, since we have confidence to enter the Most Holy Place by the blood of Jesus, by a new and living way opened for us through the curtain, that is, his body, and since we have a great priest over the house of God, let us draw near . . . in full assurance of faith, having our hearts sprinkled to cleanse us from a guilty conscience and having our bodies washed with pure water.[8]

No one who understands God, or the gospel, or themselves, will find strange the biblical stress on sin or the place of reverence and humility in true worship. In proportion, as we have exalted thoughts of God we are likely to have lowly thoughts of ourselves; in proportion, as we understand his holiness and purity we shall confess our sin and unworthiness to be called his sons and daughters,[9] but, in proportion, as we understand his love and grace in the gospel we shall accept his forgiveness and love, wear the robe and ring and share the joy of the Father's house.[10]

I have never found this more movingly put than in the hymn by Thomas Binney:

Eternal Light! Eternal Light!
How pure the soul must be,
When, placed within Thy searching sight,
It shrinks not, but with calm delight
Can live and look on Thee.

O how shall I, whose native sphere
Is dark, whose mind is dim,
Before th' Ineffable appear
And on my naked spirit bear
The uncreated dream?

There is a way for man to rise
To that sublime abode:
An offering and a sacrifice,
A Holy Spirit's energies,
An Advocate with God.

These, these prepare us for the sight
Of holiness above:
The sons of ignorance and night
May dwell in the eternal light
Through the eternal love![11]

Notes

1 Hab. 1:13.
2 See Isa. 6:3,5.
3 Isa. 63:15–16.
4 Donald Guthrie, *New Testament theology*, Leicester, IVP, 1981, p. 80.
5 Mark 14:36; Rom. 8:15; Gal. 4:6.
6 Guthrie, p. 84.
7 Heb. 4:16.
8 Heb. 10:19–22.
9 Luke 15:8.
10 Luke 15:22–4.
11 'Eternal Light, Eternal Light', Thomas Binney (1798–1874).

6

A FATHER WHO LOVES

Anyone who imagines that the Old Testament presents only a God of wrath and that it was left to the New Testament writers to discover God's love shows a pretty woeful ignorance of both! From the start of the Old Testament, and increasingly throughout its books of law and prophecy, psalms and history, we are constantly shown that love is essential to God. Carl Henry writes: 'Love is not accidental or incidental to God; it is an essential revelation of the divine nature, a fundamental and eternal perfection . . . it is the shaping principle of his creative and redeeming work!'[1]

If holy is *what* God is, love is *how* he is. Among the biblical writers no one soars higher in matters of doctrine than the apostle John. His gospel begins with one of the most sublime declarations of the person of Christ in the entire Scriptures.[2] Yet the same writer, in his first epistle, gives us an equally memorable doctrine of God the Father as light[3] and life[4] and truth[5] and, above all, as love:[6] 'God is love. Whoever lives in love lives in God, and God in him',[7] 'Whoever does not love does not know God, because God is love.'[8]

It is because he is love that we can trust him, obey him and love him in return without reserve and without conditions. It is his love which controls his power: it is his love which sets his goals and sustains his purposes of grace, it is his love which makes him accessible to us in all his perfections.

Love in God is not only a resident quality but an outgoing force. Our use of the word 'love' often tends to be dominated by the idea of romance and the concept can easily become sentimental. But the essence of love at its highest is *self-giving* and in Scripture it is this self-giving which characterises the love of God for the world. It is however a self-giving in *grace*, because when God gave himself for us we were his enemies not his friends, living in selfish rebellion, not seeking him in racial repentance for reconciliation. Paul writes in Romans:

> You see, at just the right time, when we were still powerless, Christ died for the ungodly. Very rarely will anyone die for a righteous person, though for a good person someone might possibly dare to die. But God demonstrates his own love for us in this: While we were still sinners, Christ died for us.[9]

This is precisely the extent of God's love and self-giving. When God the Father sent the Son into the world he did not stay behind, as it were, safe, invulnerable, uninvolved. In Jesus, God came; he was 'Immanuel', God with us: God in the stable and the manger, God in the carpenter's shop, God on the Galilean road and God on the cross of Calvary's hill. And while it was God the Son who became man and died for us, he was the point of vulnerability and pain for the whole God-head. 'For God so loved the world that *he gave* his one and only Son.'[10] And when God gave up his own Son he did not give someone *else* to bear our sins: he gave himself in the person of his beloved Son for 'God was reconciling the world to himself in Christ, not counting men's sins against them.'[11]

Here is the infinite God, eternally self-sufficient in power and blessedness and glory. He did not have to create the universe or this world. Yet in his love and goodness he purposed to create our world and ourselves in it, and to create us, not as bits of nature but as unique beings, known by him and made to know him. This world was made for us in all its complexity and we were made for him in all our uniqueness.[12] We were never meant to be lost in this world, anonymous in the great cosmos, dying without hope, leaving the world without knowing why we came into it.

But God's word tells us that we fell as a race, and fell

far and foully; sin has entered our history and damaged our world. It became a world of conflict and fear and failure and despair, a world dominated by sin and death. For all its beauty there was a sickness at its heart and for all our dignity there was a sickness in our heart too. And throughout our history we see war and exploitation and cruelty and disease and death even to the present day.

Yet into this world God came. He did not have to come. He could have demolished the whole thing and started again; he could have crumpled it all up, tossed it into some celestial waste-paper basket and made a new race, one which would not rebel and corrupt his creation. But he did not. Through the long centuries he 'suffered us' to go on in our ways. And often terrible ways they were too. And in that dark and primitive world he began the history of redemption: calling a man, Abraham; claiming a nation, Israel; sending the prophets to teach the true faith in a world where our religions were often as debased as we. Finally, in the fullness of time, 'God sent forth his Son', born of a woman, one utterly holy, entirely obedient human being, divine but also human, living the life that was demanded of us, 'born of a woman, born under law',[13] and then dying the death that could have been demanded of us, the death sin deserved, bearing the wrath of God, pent up through the centuries of human sin: 'God presented him as a sacrifice of atonement [which would become effective in our lives] through faith in his blood . . . he did it to demonstrate his justice at the present time, so as to be just and the one who justifies those who have faith in Jesus';[14] 'This is love: not that we loved God, but that he loved us and sent his Son as an atoning sacrifice for our sins.'[15]

In the death of Christ we find the love of God. Father, Son and Holy Spirit, in a holy conspiracy, achieved the best act of God in the worst act of humanity. There we learn what love is and see its highest demonstration.[16] There we learn that love is not merely attitude but action, not simply sympathy but movement, and as we move out into our world in love we move out with God, co-workers with the Great Lover and witness to all we meet that 'God is love'.

Notes

1 Carl Henry, *God, Revelation and Authority*, vol. 6, Waco, Texas, Word Books, 1983, p. 341.
2 John 1:1–18.
3 1 John 1:5.
4 1 John 2:24–5.
5 1 John 5:20.
6 1 John 3:1; 4:7–21.
7 1 John 4:16.
8 1 John 4:8.
9 Rom. 5:6–8.
10 John 3:16.
11 2 Cor. 5:19.
12 Gen. 1:26–8.
13 Gal. 4:4–5, with Acts 17: 22–31.
14 Rom. 3:25–6.
15 1 John 4:10.
16 John 15:12.

7

A FATHER WHO GUIDES

God has a plan for our lives: a plan drawn up by perfect love with perfect wisdom. It is not a plan like the blue-print set out on a clean sheet of paper. It is one made in the full knowledge of the confusion, tragedy, injustice and distortions of a fallen world and its effects on each of us. It is a secure plan, but drawn up with tears in prospect of the abused child, the battered mother, the wrecked career and the widespread victims of disease, accident and war. It is a battle-plan that enlists us among the armies of light and truth, of love and peace, of faith and hope in a world of superstition and despair, in a world of the half-truth and the lie, a world of selfishness and cynicism. It is also a plan which will not fail, drawn by a love that will not give up and a sovereignty that will not be denied.[1] It is a plan drawn up not only with tears but with unquenchable joy by the God who knows the end of a thing from its beginning.

Meantime he leads his child through darkness and storm, sunshine and success, setback and sorrow – to victory:

> So long Thy pow'r hath blest me, sure it still
> Will lead me on
> O'er moor and fen o'er crag and torrent 'til
> The night is gone.[2]

On our knees and on our feet, making our decisions and keeping them, we can rely on a Father who guides us, who will correct or confirm our expectations, who educates us in his school and puts us to work in his world (we go to both at the same time!). The writer of Proverbs went to that school and sought to model his wisdom on God's and to teach his 'sons' as God had taught him: 'Trust in the Lord with all your heart and lean not on your own understanding; in all your ways acknowledge him, and he will make your paths straight.'[3]

Sadly, Solomon found it easier to teach such wisdom than to practise it![4] When truth becomes theoretical we become philosophers instead of practitioners, and philosophers have been among the most foolish as well as the most wise of men. The wisdom of the Old Testament is a practical wisdom, a God-fearing obedience: 'The fear of the Lord is the beginning of wisdom.'[5]

It is of major importance in our lives that we understand that God is concerned to guide us. He is not content to be on the sidelines watching or at the end of our journey waiting. He has said clearly and firmly: 'I will instruct you and teach you in the way you should go; I will counsel you and watch over you. Do not be like the horse or the mule which have no understanding but must be controlled by bit and bridle or they will not come to you.'[6]

How often we let the pride and pressures of life control us, how often outside sources become 'bit and bridle', how often God has to steer us, his children, who are supposed to listen, in just the same way as he has to steer others who are not his children and have no intention of going his way. God's guidance is a privilege which we can and should make much of, however complicated we find it. John White is absolutely right when he says:

The heart and core of the guidance God gives is bound up in the personal relationship he wants to have with us . . . He wants to guide me. He is interested in me . . . He doesn't say 'O don't bother me now. I have the matters of the universe to look after. I have a new galaxy that I'm getting into place and it's rather tricky. Please don't come to me for guidance about something in the kitchen sink.'[7]

However just as God's concern is with every aspect of our lives, so our concern must be for his lordship over every aspect of our lives and for the will of God to be done in every part of those lives. John White gives wise counsel when he writes:

> God is not interested in guiding us about just one choice. Suppose I say to an interior decorator: 'Look at our dining room. It's a mess. Please do something about it.' But the interior decorator might respond, 'Your dining room is a mess. But the problem is that your whole life is a mess. I can't fix the dining room without also dealing with everything that is around it. Give me the whole house to decorate. I'll do the job. But don't ask me to do the dining room alone.' When we come to God asking for guidance he says 'Give me your life.' That is his priority. He does not want to guide us about a specific issue alone. 'You have that problem in your life' he says, 'because you have not given to me the whole of your life.'[8]

The most important thing in this difficult area of guidance, of decision-making, of knowing God's will, is not so much the decisions we make but the spirit in which we make them, not our calculation but our consecration. If this is right then we may still make mistakes and we may, anyway, be led to testing times and experiences, but we can trust to a Sovereign God whose providence can recover us and redirect us for 'we know that in all things God works for the good of those who love him, who have been called according to his purpose.'[9]

Often we have to proceed in life without knowing the next step or even the final (earthly!) goal. One man whose trust in the Lord led him to a great adventure was Abraham. He became father of many nations[10] but only because God became a Father to him and because he obeyed God's call, 'Leave your country, your people and your father's household and go to the land I will show you.' Someone has said that when God called Abraham out from Ur of the Chaldees, 'he did not know where he was going but he knew who he was going with!' This is what matters most for us all.

Sometimes the guiding hand and presence of our Father is hardest to discern in the delays of life, in its frustrating inactivity in sickness or unemployment. In the Bible of George Muller a marginal note was found beside the (Authorised Version) text Psalm 37 verse 23: 'The steps of a good man are ordered of the Lord' – 'and the stops too' Muller had added!

Yet in the end our Father guides us and gets us to the points, more crucial perhaps than we know, where we play a critical part in his larger purposes, his master-plan. And our part in all this is to walk in faith, in prayer and according to his Word, in common sense and with an ear for the wise counsel of friends. Then we can show the peace of a surrendered heart in safe hands.

Notes

1 John 6:37–40; Eph. 1:11.
2 'Lead kindly light', John Henry Newman (1801–1890).
3 Prov. 3:5–6.
4 1 Kgs. 11:1–6.
5 Prov. 1:7; 9:10.
6 Ps. 32:8–9.
7 John White, *The Race*, Leicester, IVP, 1984, pp. 145–7.
8 White, pp. 151–2.
9 Rom. 8:28.
10 Gen. 12:1–3; 17:4.

8

A FATHER WITH AUTHORITY

It is, no doubt, a sign of our times that the first association with the word 'Father' in Jesus' time is possibly the last we might make in our own. It is the concept of authority. In the first century, almost universally, a father had very great authority over his children and over his sons even into adulthood and marriage. True, that must have been very often misdirected or abused. But here is the best of fathers with the best of purposes directed by the highest wisdom and the purest love. In our own time the concept of authority has become so devalued that it is largely regarded as out of date and socially undesirable, interfering with individual growth and even individual freedom. What for centuries was regarded as a vital good is now regarded by many as an evil. Harry Blamires has replied well to this:

> The public mind in our generation has been confused and misled precisely by concealment of the fact that in religion, in education, in the life of society generally, it is authority that saves us from authoritarianism. It is respect for the central orthodoxies of law, culture and religion that alone preserves us from a multiplicity of intolerable petty authoritarianisms exercised by those who have the loudest voices, the strongest arms, or the most assertive egos.[1]

To repeat his assertion: 'Authority saves us from authoritarianism.' To recognise the authority of God over every sphere of life – personal, social, political – and over every decision we make – in relationships, in career, in life-style – is to place a precious human life into those hands which are best able to shape and direct it for his glory and our good.

The alternative is surrender to the pressures, demands and manipulations of others around us even while we continue to insist that we are under no authority and free from all control. In spite of our proud boast, we find over and over again that the petty tyranny of self has to give way to the stronger tyranny of others. We are saved from such a fate only by a willing surrender to the authority of 'our Father in heaven'. We are most free when most obedient, most our own when most his, we stand tall when we kneel before him.

The fatherhood of God is no 'of course' doctrine. It has implications. The implication of fatherhood is honour; the obligation of honour is obedience. This was the message of Old Testament prophets such as Malachi: '"A son honours his father, and a servant his master. If I am a father, where is the honour due to me? If I am a master, where is the respect due to me?" says the Lord Almighty.'[2]

It is impossible to give God honour without obedience. To sentimentalise this Fatherhood and sanitise it of mastery is to offer insult, not adoration. Prophets like Isaiah poured scorn on those who reduced obedience to liturgy: 'When you come to appear before me, who has asked this of you, this trampling of my courts? Stop bringing meaningless offerings! Your incense is detestable to me.'[3]

The call to hallow the name of this Father is, as we shall see in another chapter, a call to action as well as adoration: 'Stop doing wrong, learn to do right! Seek justice, encourage the oppressed. Defend the cause of the fatherless, plead the cause of the widow.'[4] These are among the much-denied 'absolutes' of life. But while we defend the existence of absolutes against the relativising which has marked much modern thought, we must realise that they are not self-existent qualities, isolated philosophical 'givens', but predicated on the character of the God who is there for everyone at all times. They are personal qualities in God and authoritative demands from God before they are ethical 'absolutes' in some abstract independent way. Such obedience as God our Father requires of us, however, is of a very special and specific type: it is to be free, grateful and above all loving. Love must be its motivation and more love its outcome; a love learned from him before given to him; a love in return for a love received. When love fuels obedience, obedience goes far – and fast: 'I run in the path of your commands, for you have set my heart free.'[5] This love in turn flows from encountering and receiving the love of God our Father: a love that cost him dear: 'For God so loved the world that he gave his one and only Son, that whoever believes in him shall not perish but have eternal life.'[6]

The implications of that are brought out by the apostle John in his first epistle: 'Dear friends, since God so loved us, we also ought to love one another . . . God is love. Whoever lives in love lives in God and God in him. In this way, love is made complete among us so that we will have confidence on the day of judgement, because in this world we are like him.'[7]

Notes

1 Harry Blamires, *Where do we stand*? London, S.P.C.K., 1980, p. 73.
2 Mal. 1:6.
3 Isa. 1:12–13.
4 Isa. 1:16–17.
5 Ps. 119:32.
6 John 3:16.
7 1 John 4:11, 16–17.

9

A FATHER WHO DISCIPLINES

Often we do not like discipline, its controls or its directions, and sometimes we actively, even passionately, resent it. In extreme cases there are children who leave home because of such disputes with parental authority and discipline; and rather more who would like to! More often there are teenagers and adults whose lives are in a mess because they did not have the loving, firm discipline which children need and parents should give. Children need discipline and discipline demands effort – on both sides. The parent who cares will make that effort. God is the model here too.

The father who cares is also a father who disciplines. God has no 'spoilt children' as we use the term. From very early times his wisdom warned indulgent parents: 'Folly is bound up in the heart of a child, but the rod of discipline will drive it far from him'[1] and marked such discipline as a necessary part of love: 'He who spares the rod hates his son, but he who loves him is careful to discipline him.'[2]

Whatever our attitudes to the practice of corporal punishment, this early principle given to us for the development of our children reflects an ingredient in God's method of developing his children, believers who are growing to maturity in character and faith. Like our children, we too are threatened by selfishness and rebelliousness; we too can become distracted by the toys of life from its responsibilities; and we should never learn our lessons if our Father did not correct us and remind us, sometimes sharply, who we belong to and what standard is expected of us: 'My son, do not make light of the Lord's discipline, and do not lose heart when he rebukes you, because the Lord disciplines those he loves, and he punishes everyone he accepts as a son.'[3]

The writer of Hebrews makes much use of this feature

in the divine fatherhood. He is writing to a community of Jewish believers who are suffering persecution at the hands of their fellow countrymen. Their early zeal and courage are diminishing. They are warned to pay 'more careful attention' to the gospel they have heard, so that they do not 'drift away':[4]

> In your struggle against sin, you have not yet
> resisted to the point of shedding your blood.
> And have you forgotten that word of encouragement
> that addresses you as sons: 'My son, do not make
> light of the Lord's discipline, and do not lose
> heart when he rebukes you, because the Lord
> disciplines those he loves, and he punishes
> everyone he accepts as a son'. Endure hardship
> as discipline; God is treating you as sons.[5]

When pressures around try to force us into silence or to persuade us into compromise, we find within ourselves fears and selfishness and disloyalties that need the rebuke of our Father as well as the encouragement to stand firm, to speak out, to hold fast to what is right and true. That is what we have here.

To say the 'Our Father' in private may give us comfort, but to serve our Father in public may well lead us to heaven through painful places. In a world which has no gods or many gods or another god than the God and Father of our Lord Jesus Christ, we too may have to 'endure hardship' and the discipline of sons.[6] But it is precisely *there* in the 'avoidable sufferings' that meet Christian faith and obedience in this world that we 'submit to the Father of our spirits'.[7]

We cannot say 'Your kingdom come' unless we say 'my kingdom goes' – and 'my ambition', 'my pride', 'my security', even 'my life'. But we cannot say 'Your will be done' through gritted teeth and with a resentful spirit, for the submission must be from within – which is to say it must be 'from above', for only by a supernatural work within us can we achieve a goal so far beyond us.

Has God 'disciplined' you? Are you suffering 'because of righteousness'?[8] Have you resented it, feared it, fought it? Did you think he *owed* you a favour? Have you learned the lesson now? Have you *submitted* to the Father? That is the decisive thing. You are not the first that he has brought to a fuller development through suffering and set-back, through initial resentment and the final realisation that the Father owes us nothing but himself and will never deny us that. His disciplines are only meant to drive us closer to himself. They do not signify rejection but its opposite. We can comfort ourselves with this and act upon it. What parent meeting a trusting hand and a tearful face, rebellion in full surrender, independence seeking reconciliation, shame seeking solace, has not drawn closer than ever the child they loved – and disciplined.

Notes

1 Prov. 22:15.
2 Prov. 13:24.
3 Heb. 12:5–6.
4 Heb. 2:1.
5 Heb. 12:4–7.
6 Heb. 12:7.
7 Heb. 12:9.
8 Matt. 5:10.

10

A FATHER WHO DELIGHTS

Parents should not only have real affection for their children but show it too, and it is always sad to meet parents who cannot say or show their feelings directly (often because *their* parents could not!). God our Father can help us break the entail of previous generations, and as Christ is more perfectly formed in us we should become more integrated and more able to express our feelings.

For some of us it is easy to show our feelings. In my home hugs are almost compulsory and although our own sons are now strapping six foot men I still insist on the occasional hugging session. Every child should know that a father does not only correct, he also cuddles, and there are times when we too feel the embrace of God warming our hearts and strengthening our spirits. It may be in solitary prayer or in a crowded celebration; it may be at a time of great distress or one of great joy; it may be as we read the Book that was written for us or admire the beauty of creation which is God's other book in which we read his power and wisdom. This is the work of the Spirit.

The Holy Spirit is God-next-to-us, it is he, the Third Person of the holy and blessed Trinity, who lives in us with immeasurable patience and care, and who works with us seeking to shape us into the likeness of Christ. Much of this work is done by him indirectly through our reading of Scripture, by means of the teaching and fellowship of the Church, in personal prayer and in our resolve to act and react as Christ would have us do.

But there are also times when, through the direct witness of the Holy Spirit, God communicates to us something of his love, his joy, his purity and his peace. Paul writes of such times: 'For you did not receive a spirit that makes you a slave again to fear, but you received the Spirit of sonship.

And by him we cry "Abba, Father". The Spirit himself testifies with our spirit that we are God's children.'[1]

We see examples of this happening with great dramatic force in the book of Acts: to the disciples on the day of Pentecost in Acts 2; to the half-Jewish Samaritans in Acts 8; to the Gentile Cornelius and his household in Acts 10; and to a group of John the Baptist's converts caught in a time warp in Acts 19. In other words, wherever the gospel about Jesus went this privilege went with it. And Church history abounds with examples that contradict attempts to restrict such direct, immediate experience of God to the New Testament times.

When the great seventeenth-century mathematician and philosopher Blaise Pascal died, they found sewn inside his shirt a piece of paper on which he had recorded what was evidently a profound and precious experience of God:

> This day of Grace 1654; From about half past ten at night, to about half after midnight, Fire. Fire. God of Abraham. God of Isaac, God of Jacob, not of the philosophers and the wise. Security, security. Feeling, joy, peace. God of Jesus Christ . . . Forgetfulness of the world and of all save God . . . Joy, joy, joy, tears of joy . . . Renunciation total and sweet.[2]

Many other such testimonies could be given in times ancient and modern, in traditions Catholic and Protestant, from writers humble and great. The New England theologian Jonathan Edwards was extraordinary because he combined one of the greatest minds of his time with the heart of a pastor and evangelist and leader in the great eighteenth-century revival (the revival in which Whitefield and the Wesleys famously participated and led here in Britain). Edwards records one of many such experiences which he had, while in meditation and prayer:

> Once as I rode out into the woods for my health in 1737, having alighted from my horse in a retired place, as my manner commonly has been, to walk for divine

contemplation and prayer, I had a view that for me was extraordinary, of the glory of the Son of God as Mediator between God and man, and his wonderful, great, pure and sweet grace and love, and meek and gentle condescension. This grace that appeared so calm and sweet appeared also great among the heavens. The Person of Christ appeared ineffably excellent, with an excellency great enough to swallow up all thought and conception, which continued, as near as I can judge, about an hour, which kept me the greater part of the time in a flood of tears and weeping aloud. I felt an ardency of soul to be, what I know not otherwise how to express, emptied and annihilated; to lie in the dust and to be full of Christ alone; to love him with a holy and pure love; to trust in him, to live upon him, to serve and follow him and to be perfectly sanctified and made pure with a divine and heavenly purity.[3]

Many others of that time and since have recorded such experiences of God's closeness and love: 'Love fell in showers on my soul' recorded Howell Harris;[4] 'I felt my heart strangely warmed' testified the very rational John Wesley;[5] 'God revealed himself to me, and I had such an experience of his love that I had to ask him to stay his hand' wrote the nineteenth-century evangelist D.L. Moody years after his experience.[6] An older contemporary of Moody, Charles Finney, records his own experience:

The Holy Spirit descended upon me in a manner that seemed to go through me, body and soul. No words can express the wonderful love that was shed abroad in my heart. I wept aloud with joy and love . . . These waves came over me and over me and over me one after another until I recollect I cried out 'I shall die if the waves continue to pass over me.' I said 'Lord I cannot bear any more' yet I had no fear of death.[7]

Church history past and present is full of such testimonies. It is sadly true, however, that such experiences are all too rare for most of us, even in much lower degree. God's dealings with us in this world are still to a degree conditioned by its fallen-ness and we do not see or feel him as we would wish. Yet if such experiences are possible on earth how glorious will be his intimacies in heaven!

Notes

1 Rom. 8:15–16.
2 D.M. Lloyd-Jones, *Joy Unspeakable*, Eastbourne, Kingsway Publications, 1984, pp. 106–7.
3 Jonathan Edwards (1703–1758), see Lloyd-Jones, pp. 79–80.
4 Howell Harris (1714–1773), see D.M. Lloyd-Jones, *Romans. An Exposition of Chapter 8: 5–17 The Sons of God*, Edinburgh, The Banner of Truth Trust, 1974, p. 349.
5 John Wesley (1703–1791), *The Journal*, ed. N. Curnock, vol. 1, London, Robert Culley, n.d., entry for May 14th 1738, p. 476.
6 D.L. Moody (1837–1899), see Lloyd-Jones, *Joy Unspeakable*, p. 80.
7 Charles Finney (1792–1875), *Charles G. Finney. An Autobiography*, London, The Salvation Army, n.d., pp. 17, 18.

11

A FATHER TO BE IMITATED

A holy God calls for a holy people; a holy Father may expect to see his family likeness in all his children. As he said long ago to his people Israel, 'Be holy because I am holy',[1] so he says now to the whole Israel of God, Jew and Gentile believers, ourselves included: 'As obedient children, do not conform to the evil desires you had when you lived in ignorance. But just as he who called you is holy, so be holy in all you do; for it is written "Be holy, because I am holy."'[2]

This is the foundation of Christian ethics. We hear absolutes denied and affirmed around us; but even for the Christian, ethical absolutes are not things that exist apart from God, floating free in the universe like elusive particles. It is God's holy character, his goodness and truth, his purity and wisdom, which are the source and test of all that is good. When Moses, that servant of God, begged his Master 'Now show me your glory', the reply of Yahweh was 'I will cause all my goodness to pass in front of you.'[3] In the event God proclaimed his 'name', that is his nature, and did so in terms of a moral and spiritual relationship and its demands and penalties. 'The Lord, the Lord, the compassionate and gracious God, slow to anger, abounding in love and faithfulness, maintaining love to thousands and forgiving wickedness, rebellion and sin. Yet he does not leave the guilty unpunished.'[4]

All the human virtues of justice and mercy, love and faithfulness, have their rise, not in the social convenience of human society, but, before that, in the being of God and thence in the constitution and consciences of men and women made in his image.

Jesus taught his followers that for them these standards were not impracticable ideals but substantial possibilities.

While others retained and reflected something of God's moral judgements and characteristics because they were his creation, believers could reach and practise a higher perfection because they were his children: 'Love your enemies and pray for those who persecute you, that you may be [i.e. consistently] sons of your Father in heaven . . . If you love those who love you . . . Do not even pagans do that? Be perfect, therefore, as your heavenly Father is perfect.'[5]

Jesus himself is the perfect model of that but gives his followers power too, to put into life what others put into poetry: to *live out* human ideals and divine commands by living *in him* in obedience and fruitfulness. 'I am the vine; you are the branches. If a man remains in me and I in him, he will bear much fruit . . . You are my friends if you do what I command . . . I have called you friends, for everything that I learned from my Father I have made known to you.'[6]

Paul uses a strikingly familiar word when he writes to the Ephesian Christians: 'Be *imitators* of God, therefore, as dearly loved children and live a life of love, just as Christ loved us and gave himself up for us as a fragrant offering and sacrifice to God.'[7] His word 'imitators' is the word from which we get our word 'mimics'; yet it is no mere mimicry that he calls us to, but the cultivation of family traits and the practice of family ways 'as dearly loved children'. And, as everywhere, Christ is the model, and the mainspring of this is his perfect life and reconciling death. We belong to God because of him, we are related to him as our Elder Brother,[8] and the great and final work of God is to conform us 'to the likeness of his Son, that he might be the firstborn among many brothers.'[9]

The imitation of God does not lie only in the cultivation of inner qualities but also in our public interaction with others. As the apostle Paul teaches the Ephesian Christians, it involves love in real life situations,[10] resistance of life's seductions,[11] the contradiction of surrounding darkness,[12] and the challenge of what is with what can be.[13] It is an imitation which comes into its own in situations of loving commitment such as marriage[14] and family loyalty[15] and in situations of trust and responsibility.[16] In the words of John: 'God is love. Whoever lives in love lives in God, and God in him. In this way, love is made complete among us so that we will have confidence on the day of judgement, because in this world we are like him.'[17]

Notes

1 Lev. 11:44–5.
2 1 Pet. 1:14–15.
3 Exod. 33:18–19.
4 Exod. 34:6–7.
5 Matt. 5:44, 46–8.
6 John 15:5, 14–15.
7 Eph. 5:1.
8 John 20:17.
9 Rom. 8:28; cf. Eph. 2:10.
10 Eph. 5:2.
11 Eph. 5:3–7.
12 Eph. 5:8–12.
13 Eph. 5:13–14.
14 Eph. 5:22–33.
15 Eph. 6:1–4.
16 Eph. 6:5–9.
17 1 John 4:16–17.

12

WORSHIP AS ADORATION

Hallowed be your name

'To hallow' means to treat as holy. It denotes reverence and suggests worship. God's name in biblical language stands for his nature with its qualities and powers. To hallow God's name therefore is to hold him in reverence, to worship and obey him. It is to respond to what he has revealed of himself, in appropriate ways; it is to adore his person, to respect his judgements and to follow his ways. To pray 'hallowed be your name' is to begin the process of worship.

What is worship? Our word comes from the Anglo-Saxon 'worth-ship', which means ascribing worth to God. He is worthy of all honour and praise, attention and obedience; and worship includes all of these. One of the finest and most well-known definitions of worship is that given by William Temple:

> Worship is the submission of all our nature to God. It is the quickening of the conscience by His holiness; the nourishment of the mind with His truth; the purifying of the imagination by His beauty; the opening of the heart to His love; the surrender of the will to His purpose – and all this gathered up in adoration, the most selfless emotion of which our nature is capable and therefore the chief remedy for that self-centredness which is original sin and the source of all actual sin.[1]

There are two parts to worship which make it what it is. Both are necessary to the very *being* of true worship. They are adoration and action.

We have known too little of adoration in recent times. Our secular–humanist Western society has long put man in the place of God. But our idols are letting us down. We are beginning to see that it is not only their feet which are made of clay. David Walsh writes:

> A shift of far-reaching significance is presently taking place within Western civilisation . . . No longer can we naively subscribe to the fundamental conceit from which modernity began: that human beings are capable of providing their own moral and political order . . . That experiment has run its course. Having been brought to its limits in the twentieth century, its bankruptcy has become fully exposed . . . human beings have again begun to look toward the source of order that lies beyond the self. A remarkable opening of the soul is taking place as we increasingly come to realise that we are not the self-sufficient ground of our own existence.[2]

The tragedy is that we now see many in this 'post-modern' generation turning from new idols to old ones, from scientisms to superstitions; turning to New Age religion with its hybrid mix of ideas from Hinduism, Buddhism and Western occultism, its fads of astrology, reincarnation, 'life-forces' and mystical experiences. Here all is one, all is God and we are God. But how lonely and desolate it leaves so many: as disillusioned as ever with the 'gods' they invent!

Nevertheless a power above all created powers – real or imagined – does call to men and women: a power personal and good, holy and true; the God 'who waits to be gracious'. In immeasurable contrast to all idols and other rivals it is the greatness and goodness, the majesty and grace, the power and love of God that inspires us to adore him in silent contemplation and in joyful song, in the tongues of men and of angels, alone and among the communities of the redeemed. And he does not call for adoration as a bribe, nor only as his due, but as something which is both his right and our fulfilment. We only find ourselves when we find the one true God. Our freedom lies in renouncing our independence and acknowledging his authority and rule. Only as we hallow his name do we remember our own:

> Immortal, invisible, God only wise,
> In light inaccessible hid from our eyes,
> Most blessed, most glorious, the Ancient of Days,
> Almighty, victorious, Thy great name we praise.[3]

One of the most profoundly moving discoveries for me was the knowledge that I can actually give God my Father pleasure in worship: that he can say to me as the Lover says to the Beloved in the Song of Solomon: 'Show me your face, let me hear your voice; for your voice is sweet and your face is lovely.'[4] It seems so surprising knowing the poverty of all I have to offer him. But it is true for me and for all of us in his family. No fond parent ever sought out more their own child in a school choir or pageant than *your* divine and best parent seeks *you* out today and calls *you* to sing, to pray, to listen and to respond in love and obedience. You may consider yourself to be just one of the crowd but to your maker, redeemer and friend you are quite irreplaceable.

> Yet I may love Thee, too, O Lord
> Almighty as Thou art,
> For Thou hast stooped to ask of me
> The love of my poor heart.[5]

The great spur to this in our church services must be, of course, the fact and the knowledge of the presence of God our Father in the midst of his people. We come to church to meet God – nothing less than that. And out of that meeting comes his glory and his praise on earth and our awe and adoration of him, our hope and our joy. As Siegfried Grossman writes: 'Every genuine religious experience is in essence an experience of the *presence* of God . . . of contact in the here and now with the overwhelming, joy-bringing, terrifying, saving and judging power of the transcendent.'[6]

We must have adoration in our Christian service and experience. There must be times when God so fills the horizon that for a time other things fall back and fade and we can contemplate God alone: marvelling at the mystery of his being and love, listening to his wisdom as he speaks in uncluttered moments, renewing our vows, and laying our lives gratefully and unresistingly in his hands.

> And thus looking within and around me
> I ever renew
> (With the stoop of the soul which in
> bending upraises it too)
> The submission of man's nothing-perfect
> to God's all-complete,
> As by each new obeisance in spirit, I
> climb to his feet.[7]

A sight of God is a breath-taking thing. It can come in silence or in song, in reading, prayer or sermon: a sight of God in his infinite perfection: 'Infinite, eternal and unchangeable in His being, wisdom, power, holiness, justice, goodness and truth.'[8]

But there is no sight of God to equal a sight of God in Christ, his Son and image. Ours is a Trinitarian faith and our worship must have its Trinitarian dimensions. Among men and angels there was no one who could say 'Anyone who has seen me has seen the Father', or insist that all must 'honour the Son just as they honour the Father'.[9] In the sinless Son we see the Holy Father, and in the Son's self-giving on the cross we see as nowhere else the integrity of the Father's righteousness and the extent of the Father's love. At his cradle, at his cross and at his empty tomb, as well as now in the glory of his Father, the call is given to us all:

O come let us adore him
Christ the Lord.

The place of the Holy Spirit in all this is no less crucial. Without his illumination our minds are dark with ignorance and prejudice, without his convicting and softening power our hearts are proud and hard, without his fellowship channelling to us grace from the Son and love from the Father our lives remain unchanged and our hearts empty of God. But by the Spirit God comes in to fill us with the sense of God around us. It is the Spirit who takes us to worship, who opens us up to God and who keeps these times of grace effective in our memories and daily lives. It is because of this ministry that St. Bernard of Clairvaux could say: 'I never come to thee but by thee: I never go from thee without thee.'[10]

Notes

1 William Temple (1881–1944).
2 David Walsh, *After Ideology*, San Francisco, Harper, 1990, p. 1.
3 'Immortal, invisible, God only wise', Walter Chalmers Smith (1824–1908).
4 S. of S. 2:14.
5 'My God, how wonderful Thou art', F.W. Faber (1814–63).
6 Siegfried Grossman (quoting Ernst Benz) in *Stewards of God's Grace*, trans. M. Freeman, Exeter, Paternoster, 1977, p. 64.
7 Robert Browning, 'Saul', *The Poems of Robert Browning*, London, O.U.P., 1964, p. 230.
8 The Westminster Shorter Catechism, 1648, Question 4, 'What is God?'
9 John 14:9; John 5:23.
10 St. Bernard of Clairvaux (1090–1153).

13

WORSHIP AS ACTION

Adoration without action is in biblical faith unthinkable and incomprehensible. Worship, which is true and acceptable, involves the whole of a person (not just the mind or 'soul') and the whole of life (not just the supposedly-sacred time or space of special days and special places). As Miroslav Volf writes: 'There is no space in which worship should not take place, no time when it should not occur, and no activity in which it should not happen.'[1] True Christian worship is 'worldly' and physical as well as 'churchly' and spiritual. That is, it involves life in the body and in the world: 'Therefore I urge you, brothers, in view of God's mercy, to offer your bodies as living sacrifices, holy and pleasing to God – this is your spiritual act of worship.'[2]

It is true we need special times when we can stand apart from the pressures and distractions of life and when we can enter the experience of worshipping with others of the Christian community in order to be built up in faith and prepared for good works. But the out-working of what we learn and receive in the church meetings in the week before us and the world around us is *integral to* as well as crucial for true spiritual worship.

As the reader will have seen by now, I am a preacher, and a few years ago a good friend of mine, Revd Dr R.T. Kendall, asked me to speak to his lunch-time service in Westminster Chapel for people who work in that area of London. As my short address to those business men and women says much of what I want to say here, I have incorporated it into this book hoping that even if some of the geographical references are obscure to some readers the message will be plain, and also perhaps more forceful in its original form. The talk was entitled: *The Altar and the Office Desk*.

Let me begin at the end. What I want to show is not merely that there is a connection between the desk and the altar, but that from Monday to Friday the desk *is* the altar.

I meet too many Christians who are fired up on Sunday and deflated by Wednesday because they feel their job is somehow second best in the Christian life. Sometimes they talk wistfully of going into something called 'full-time Christian service', never thinking that what they are already doing *is* full-time Christian service because they are full-time Christian servants. Mark you, what they are presently engaged in may be *poor* full-time Christian service but probably only because they are poor full-time Christian servants – sloppy or selective or crotchety or unprincipled! The idea that one vocation is more holy than another is pre-Reformation. The continental Reformers and English Puritans of the sixteenth and seventeenth centuries baptised every occupation as a divine calling, an ordained and strategic employment in which God could be glorified. So should we all.

The eager young professional, however, often feels he or she cannot give God the pre-eminence he deserves or serve his kingdom in the job they do. They could be door-to-door evangelising among the shabby high-rise buildings on the Isle of Ely, but they have been seconded to the office blocks of Westminster. They could be hacking their way through the jungle of the Amazon or the forests of Zaïre (pith helmets provided) instead of taking the 7.00 a.m. commuter train from Haywards Heath. Christian magnificence, they are sure, consists of wasting away in Nepal, not growing fat on luncheon vouchers in Petty France.

But wait a minute, if God has called you to Petty France, what business have you in Nepal? And if you are already on your way, how soon will you be back to continue in the Lord's work? To come a little nearer home, I have seen successful men enter the pastoral ministry who were never successful there or thereafter. They dreamed a dream and forgot to wake up; they got a call and lost their calling. It was such a pity, such a waste. Better to be a better banker than a boring preacher; better to fill an export order than to empty a church.

It has always been a masterly piece of strategy on Satan's part to convince Christian people that the nearer you live to God, the more you withdraw from the world. This leaves his own territory unchallenged and unthreatened. Christian faith and spirituality is relegated to the harmless play-area of private life. Even the conscientious 9 to 5 man can find himself living in two worlds: that of the office and that of the altar. Solid as a rock, steady as a well-rooted tree in his local church, it may well be that he experiences little buffeting from Satan because he poses little threat to Satan's kingdom – at least he is unlikely to do much damage *in the place where he can do most damage*, which is not perhaps in the local neighbourhood where he lives but in the multi-national where he works. Our greatest need is not for more Christians, not even for more Christians in the 'right' places – we have plenty there as well as elsewhere – the greatest need is for Christians to be *what* they are *where* they are: perceptively, patiently, determinedly, even fiercely.

Revolutionaries are no threat segregated from the society they want to change. A desert island is the perfect place for them! And Christians are no great threat to Satan's kingdom and no great use to Christ's huddled in house groups back home or massed in celebrations and festivals, if their Christian standards of justice, righteousness and truth do not challenge assumptions and redirect policies in their city life and business. Moonlighting for God in the twilight world of weekends at the local church is no substitute for 'full-time Christian service' in the finance company or the insurance broker's. If your 'real self' does not live in the 'real world' then it's in for an identity crisis. For which really is the true 'you', you at the prayer meeting or you at the office; you with the Bible or you with the bank statements; you in theology or you in commerce? Have you become a commuter between the world and the kingdom of God? The explosion comes when the kingdom of God *enters* the world, challenges Satan in his stronghold, plots his downfall and the eradication of structures of evil: inequity, oppression or discrimination.

It may be a surprise to some of us to learn that in the New Testament 'worship' is associated more with what we do *after* the church meetings than in them! In Romans chapter 12 what Paul describes as 'your spiritual [or reasonable, even logical] act of worship' is not the performance of a liturgy or the enjoyment of fellowship and good preaching but the dedication to God of our *bodily* existence in the day-to-day world. It is as we make the office desk the altar, the factory floor our consecrated ground, our own self-giving to the world (not simply the Church) our aim, that we most truly 'offer our bodies as living sacrifices holy and pleasing to God'.[2]

This perspective does not make 'going to church' redundant; it only makes it preparatory. It is not an end in itself but a means to an end; a ministry of encouragement which builds up the Body of Christ on earth to speak and live for him. The chief end of man is to glorify God – not in a vacuum, not in the abstract, but in the world of concrete re-alities which is God's world and which needs most of all the concrete realities of the good news of Christ Jesus.

'When does the service begin?' whispered a visitor to someone sitting beside him in a Quaker meeting. 'Just after the meeting ends!' was the reply.

Notes

1 Miroslav Volf, 'Worship as Adoration and Action in Worship' in *Adoration and Action*, ed. D.A. Carson, Carlisle, Paternoster Press, 1993, p. 204.
2 Rom. 12:1.

YOUR NAME IS MY ADDRESS!

Hallowed be your name

'So forget about yourself And concentrate on him And worship him.'[1] So says the song we often sing when we gather for worship. But it's not easy to reverse the habit of years when we concentrated not on 'him' but on ourselves and forgot about our maker who was also rightly our master. Our aim was happiness not holiness; but the further we went from holiness the further we went from happiness too! The more we centred on self the bigger grew the hole in the middle of our life. Selwyn Hughes has said: 'In all the years I have worked as a minister and a Christian counsellor I have never met a happy self-centred person. The self-centred are the unhappy and the frustrated. They express themselves but then they don't like the self they express.'[2]

In our own times we have raised self-centredness from a list of the vices to a list of the virtues. The American psychologist and Christian Paul Vitz protests against the glorification of the self evident in much Western culture and life today:

The relentless and single-minded search for and glorification of the self is at direct cross-purposes with the Christian injunction to *lose* the self. Certainly Jesus Christ neither lived nor advocated a life that would qualify by today's standards as 'self-actualised'. For the Christian self is the problem, not the potential paradise. Understanding this problem involves an awareness of sin, especially of the sin of pride; correcting this condition requires the practice of such unself-actualised states as contrition and penitence, humility, obedience and trust in God.[3]

It is when we begin to look away from ourselves to God, to transfer our ultimate loyalty from us to him, to say 'Hallowed be *your* name' that our own healing and true self-fulfilment begin. It is part of the upside-down world of God's kingdom that as we lose ourselves in this way we find ourselves. Jesus said, 'If anyone would come after me, he must deny himself and take up his cross daily and follow me. For whoever wants to save his life will lose it, but whoever loses his life for me will save it.'[4]

To deny oneself is not merely to give up things, whether sugar for Lent or smoking for good. To deny oneself is to deny the *centrality* of the self which denies and disputes the centrality of God. Self-denial is not an unnatural self-hatred, for there is a natural and proper self-love (hence we are to love our neighbour as ourselves).[5] Nor does Christian self-denial require a masochistic or wasteful suppression of personality or gifts (which are God-given and helpful to others). It is the glorification of self, the deification of self, the tyranny of self over all who challenge its supremacy which is the enemy.

It is this self-centredness, that rivals God, which he opposes and seeks to destroy. It is a corruption deep in the heart of the best of us and one which is exposed in its ugliness more and more as God comes near and lays claim on our lives. John Calvin, the great Swiss reformer, begins his famous *Institutes of the Christian Religion* with the statement: 'Nearly all the wisdom we possess, that is to say true and sound wisdom, consists of two parts: the knowledge of God and of ourselves.'[6] He goes on to show how these are crucially linked so that 'it is certain that man never achieves clear knowledge of himself, unless he has first looked upon God's face, and then descends from contemplating him to scrutinise himself.'[7] The first result of this in terms of self-knowledge he presents in uncompromising terms: 'For we always seem to ourselves righteous and upright and wise and holy – this pride is innate in all of us – unless by clear proof we stand convinced of our own unrighteousness, foulness, folly and impurity.'[8]

The most dramatic biblical illustrations of this are Isaiah and Job. The young prophet Isaiah, confronted with the vision of God in the beauty of holiness, cries out, 'Woe to me, I am ruined! For I am a man of unclean lips, and I live among a people of unclean lips, and my eyes have seen the King, the Lord Almighty.'[9] And Job responds similarly: 'My ears had heard of you but now my eyes have seen you. Therefore I despise myself and repent in dust and ashes.'[10]

We see then that the only true self-image comes from looking at God and not at ourselves. This is surely the most crucial of all factors in self-understanding and self-assessment. However we ought not to stop with Isaiah or Job's initial experience. For the love of God raises those whom the holiness of God slays, and only pride stays in the dust.

Like the father in the parable of the prodigal son,[11] his forgiveness is so complete that he brings us out of infamy into privilege, gives us beauty for ashes, turns despair into joy. In grace he not only forgives us, he changes us, not only changes us but adopts us. He gives us not merely a fresh start but a new identity and a new relationship; one which is unbreakable and which will challenge sin and backsliding, encourage godliness in all its forms and enable us to say: 'I have been crucified with Christ and I no longer live, but Christ lives in me. The life I live in the body, I live by faith in the Son of God, who loved me and gave himself for me.'[12] It is this spirit which in grateful adoration says 'Hallowed be your name.'

When we find God we find ourselves, our real worth, our true home. True, there has to be a full confession and a genuine renunciation of sin, there has to be a sloughing-off of the old attitudes of life-style. The father of the returning prodigal son called for the best robe, but first there would have been the burning of the old rags. The ring for the finger and the sandals for the feet were put on a washed body. The celebration was in the father's home, not in the far-off pigsty. It is not in 'the distant country' far from God that we find out who we are, but in the Father's house and at the Father's feet and in the Father's arms. Enlightenment intellectuals of the eighteenth century said, with Descartes, 'I think therefore I am'; primitive tribespeople find their identity in the group and say, 'I belong therefore I am', but the Christian looks up to God and says, 'I respond therefore I am':[13] 'Hallowed be *your* name.'

Notes

1 'We have come into this place', Bruce Ballinger, 1976, Word Music (UK).
2 Selwyn Hughes, The Christian Councellor's Pocket Guide, Eastbourne, Kingsway, 1982.
3 Paul Vitz, *Psychology as Religion*, Tring, Lion, 1977, p. 81.
4 Luke 9:24–5.
5 Luke 10:27.
6 John Calvin, *Institutes [Instructions] of the Christian Religion*, vol. I, Philadelphia, The Westminster Press, 1977, p. 35.
7 Calvin, p. 37.
8 Calvin, p. 37.
9 Isa. 6:5.
10 Job 42:5–6.
11 Luke 15:11–32.
12 Gal. 2:20.
13 See Tony Walter, *All you love is need*, London, S.P.C.K, 1985, pp. 154–5.

II. YOUR KINGDOM COME, YOUR WILL BE DONE ON EARTH AS IT IS IN HEAVEN

15

A WORLD IN REBELLION

Every Valentine's Day my wife, Valerie, and I chuckle over the messages which appear in *The Times*. Endless Tiggers and Poohs writing soppy notes to one another make for light relief amidst grim news. One message was not to a lover from a lover, but from grown-up children to their parents. In a touching tribute and a winsom confession they wrote: 'The rebels failed, for our Utopia was the home we fought to leave.'

It seemed to me then, as now, that that is the most perfect description of our race and its world in its long history of rebellion and independence from its creator and law-giver. We are a race of rebels doggedly determined to go it alone and to build our kingdoms; to pursue our own plans, in our own strength and according to our own rules. It has been like this almost from the beginning. The essence of Adam and Eve's sin as told in the book of Genesis was rebellion. Their creator and law-giver had given them both freedom and boundaries, lordship and limits.[1] Their rebellion involved an attempt to take their freedom beyond its boundaries, to extend the lordship they had been given until it rivalled that of God who gave it.[2] Pride and foolishness, selfishness and the lust for power all combined in the germinal sin which seeded the race thereafter and left us to bitter harvest in every age and generation. That rebellion against God which disputes his right to rule over us and shape our lives is born with us and remains in each of us, the boast of the arrogant and the shame of the humble, the 'strength' of the unbeliever and the weakness of the Christian.

What is true of the individual is writ large in our societies. Very often the New Testament writers, and especially John, speak about 'the world' in contrast to the people or Church of God, and warn believers of a deep alienation, a profound antipathy and a dangerous conflict between the two:

> Do not love the world or anything in the world.
> If anyone loves the world, the love of the Father is not in him. For everything in the world – the cravings of sinful man, the lust of his eyes and the boasting of what he has and does – comes not from the Father but from the world. The world and its desires pass away, but the man who does the will of God lives for ever.[3]

By his term 'the world' John means society constructed so as to keep God out of its affairs, society in its determined and deliberate Godlessness; it includes human politics, economics, ethics and life-style determined from within and without reference to God's character and will. When John tells us not to love 'anything in the world' he is using strong language, not with regard to our society's excellences and achievements, practical or aesthetic, but with regard to its priorities and motivations in which God is refused his place of sovereignty and judgement. Since the Fall of the race human societies rich and poor, sophisticated and ignorant, ancient and modern including our own, have shared in this conspiracy to keep God out of their affairs.

There have been many substitutes for this kingdom, ancient and modern. They have all failed. Malcolm Muggeridge in one of his books recalls his years as a young journalist, full of hope in the politics of the day. Then he had gone to Moscow in the early 1930s and had come face to face with the terrible realities around him. He writes:

> How marvellous the Russian revolution seemed when it happened! A little bearded man wearing a cap, Lenin, had taken over the vast empire of the Tsars on behalf of the workers and peasants . . . The words of the

Magnificat had been fulfilled, certainly, the mighty had been put down from their seats and the humble and meek exalted, and now I had to face the unpalatable fact that the humble and meek, thus exalted, had become mighty in their turn and fit to be put down.[4]

The enemy of all our politics is ourselves; our ideology and social engineering can never, despite all our immense resources, get the weakness and wickedness out of our hearts. Only God can do that – and he does not do it to order! Most of us want the inconveniences of sin rather than sin itself to be dealt with, but it is only on bended knee that we enter the kingdom, in full confession and sincere faith, humbling self and exalting God, in full surrender to his lordship and his love.

This analysis is pointed up in the apostle Paul's devastating indictment of the Gentile world of his own day. Once again pride, sophistication and arrogance had combined to keep the true God out of human affairs: 'They exchanged the truth of God for a lie' and the result was social alienation, sexual deviation and personal disintegration,[5] fissuring with cracks the strong and stately edifice of the Roman Empire.

At its close the New Testament canon includes the book of Revelation where this theme reaches its climax. In vivid images of beasts rising from sea and land, the growth of empires and civilisations which are hostile to God and the gospel of his Son is predicted, with only the second coming of Christ to judgement bringing the hostility to an end and establishing God's reign on earth: 'The kingdom of the world has become the kingdom of our Lord and of his Christ, and he will reign for ever and ever.'[6]

Meantime the people of God wait and work and witness in an environment hostile to their faith and first loyalty, and cry daily to God as they witness its blasphemies and its cruelties domestic and international: 'Your kingdom come'.

Notes

1 Gen. 1:28; 2:17.
2 Gen. 3:5.
3 1 John 2:15–17.
4 Malcolm Muggeridge, *Tread softly, for you tread on my jokes*, Fontana, pp. 22–3.
5 Rom. 1:28–31.
6 Rev. 11:15.

16

A GOD IN ACTION

The history of the Bible is the history of salvation, the history of God in action for the salvation of the human race. The book of Genesis is the book of beginnings: the beginning of the universe, the beginning of our world, the beginning of humankind, the beginning of sin in our world – and the beginning of redemption. We learn that God's promise is as old as his curse[1] and that no sooner had the race made in his image rebelled and began to disintegrate[2] than God began a process of rescue and reversal: gathering together and to himself a people who would 'call on the name of the Lord'[3] and live with righteousness and justice on the earth.[4] Through global judgement (the Flood) and international chaos (Babel and after) that process continued. At times God's purposes seemed about to fail. But 'is anything too hard for the Lord?'[5]

The call of Abraham began the most important stage in Old Testament salvation history. It narrowed God's purposes down to a single people but only in order to broaden those purposes out to embrace all peoples:

> The Lord had said to Abraham 'Leave your country, your people and your father's household and go to the land I will show you. I will make you into a great nation and I will bless you; I will make your name great, and you will be a blessing. I will bless those who bless you, and whoever curses you I will curse; and all peoples on earth will be blessed through you.'[6]

The family of Abraham becomes the tribes of Israel, enslaved in Egypt but 'redeemed' from bondage and led out by Moses in the great redemptive act of the exodus. At Sinai the twelve tribes become the chosen nation, the people and bride of Yahweh; a nation 'set apart' (as the word 'holy' basically means) for God. Moses leads them to the borders of their Promised Land but it is Joshua who leads them into it. In spite of her frequent tendency to forget her high calling and to compromise with the heathen nations around, God preserves Israel's identity by means of the Law given to Moses and sternly reminds the nation of her unique calling through the prophets. In their lives and in their message the prophets embody the 'faithful remnant' who stay true to the nation's life and calling.

However their prophetic messages of exposure and judgement were to them 'the burden of the Lord' which often weighed heavily upon their hearts, for they lived in hard times. This burden was only lightened by the vision of a better time which lay in the future, when God would come to the world and to his people in final judgement and salvation to establish his own rule of righteousness and peace once and for all, not only in Israel but throughout the whole earth.

Isaiah most famously and most beautifully speaks of that time.

He does so for instance in the Christmas readings of chapters 9 and 11 when he points to the child whose name will be called 'Wonderful Counsellor' and 'Prince of Peace', whose government will never end, on whom the Spirit of the Lord will rest and who will judge the world with righteousness so that 'the earth will be full of the knowledge of the Lord as the waters cover the sea.'[7]

In that day nations long hostile to one another will be at peace, for the one true God will be their unity.[8] Israel will come into her own[9] and the nations will share her God and her glory[10] in a new heaven and a new earth.[11] This time of widespread judgement and world renewal is called in the Old Testament writings 'The Day of the Lord'; and associated with it is the kingdom of God which that day ushers in.

'The kingdom of God in the Bible,' writes George

Beasley-Murray, 'primarily means God exercising his sovereign power in judgement and salvation.'[12] As the Dutch theologian, Herman Ridderbos, put it: it is 'the kingly self-assertion of God in justice and in mercy'.[13] In a word it is the rule of God in the reign of grace. Notice that God's 'kingdom' in all this is not an *area* over which he rules but an *activity* in which he extends his rule. Perhaps it would be better therefore to understand this part of the Lord's Prayer: 'Your Kingship come'.

The most important single thing about the Old Testament teaching concerning the kingdom is that Yahweh comes *in person* to do this. The coming of the kingdom is unthinkable without the coming of the King. It is by divine intervention, not social evolution, that the age of peace and prosperity dawns. As I once heard it put, the kingdom is God 'kinging it' among us!

Notes

1 Gen. 3:15.
2 Gen. 4:8.
3 Gen. 4:25–6.
4 Gen. 6:9.
5 Gen. 18:14.
6 Gen. 12:1–3.
7 Isa. 9:6,7; 11:2,9.
8 Isa. 2: 1–3; 19:19–25.
9 Isa. 52:1–2, 7.
10 Isa. 60:1–3.
11 Isa. 65:17.
12 George Beasley-Murray, *The Coming of God*, Exeter, Paternoster Press, 1983, p. 14.
13 Herman Ridderbos, *The Coming of the Kingdom*, Philadelphia, The Presbyterian and Reformed Publishing Company, 1976, p. 19.

17

THE COMING OF THE KING

When Jesus appeared on the public scene proclaiming in Galilee and preaching in the synagogues, 'The time has come [or is fulfilled], the kingdom of God is near [or is at hand],'[1] there was enormous interest and excitement. Jesus was proclaiming *the beginning* of God's long-promised intervention in human affairs, the promised restoration of all things, the final judgement and salvation of God. It is equally clear that from the start Jesus connected this kingdom with *himself*. In the synagogue at Nazareth he said after reading the first two verses of Isaiah 61: 'Today this scripture is fulfilled in your hearing.'

He went to Nazareth, where he had been brought up, and on the Sabbath day he went into the synagogue, as was his custom. And he stood up to read. The scroll of the prophet Isaiah was handed to him. Unrolling it he found the place where it is written:

'The Spirit of the Lord is on me, because he has anointed me to preach good news to the poor. He has sent me to proclaim freedom for the prisoners and recovery of sight for the blind, to release the oppressed, to proclaim the year of the Lord's favour.'[2]

Jesus was reading from one of the prophecies of universal restoration in Isaiah. In the politically charged atmosphere of early first-century Galilee, however, it would have been regarded as one of the revolutionary prophecies of the Old Testament. There the announcement 'The kingdom of heaven is at hand' would have been heard by many as equivalent to 'The revolution is about to begin'! Throughout his public ministry Jesus was alive to this tendency as well as to popular expectations that the Messiah would lead Israel, God's chosen people, to throw off the Roman yoke.

In Nazareth Jesus creates growing consternation and fury as he in fact modifies the reading from Isaiah, *leaving out* some of the very things they want to be emphasised. He reads of 'the year of the Lord's favour', but not 'the day of vengeance of our God'; he inserts an extra line from Isaiah 58:6, 'freedom for the prisoners', but not what follows, 'and break every yoke'. As Joachim Jeremias and others have pointed out, the Greek of verse 22 could be translated very differently from our popular versions and can read 'All *protested* [the Greek verb is literally 'all bore witness' and can mean to affirm or to witness against someone] with one voice and were *furious* [the Greek verb can mean amazed or horrified!] because he spoke [only] about mercy.'[3] He finally snaps the slender thread of patience in his hearers by referring to God's compassion for the Gentiles, sometimes even giving them priorities over his own Jewish people.[4] The amazement and anger at Nazareth was occasioned by Jesus announcing the revolution but not vengeance on Israel's enemies! It was a revolution of mercy, peace and blessing: to Jew and Gentile alike. This was not yet the Day of Judgement but 'the year of the Lord's favour'.

In the three years of his public ministry Jesus continued to preach the kingdom of God *and to practise its presence* in words, works and wonders. 'The foundational element in the teaching of Jesus relating to the Kingdom of God,' writes George Beasley-Murray, 'is that Jesus affirms its presence in the world in and through his word and work.'[5,6]

The sovereign work of Yahweh, which was to defeat all evil and overcome all opposition and achieve a transformed earth, had been decisively inaugurated by Jesus in his powerful deeds and authoritative words. Hence, Jesus could speak interchangeably of 'my father's kingdom' and 'my kingdom'. We read of 'the kingdom of our God and his Christ'.[7] Where God reigns, Christ Jesus his Son is

King. But what king was ever like this? Many kingdoms have been built on the blood of their enemies, but here is a kingdom which will be built on the blood of its founder and King; a kingdom won not by self-assertion but by self-surrender,[8] a kingdom whose king is its universal servant,[9] an 'upside-down kingdom' which would challenge every assumption, search every conscience and change every life it touched.

Richard Bauckham sums up the significance and effect of Jesus's kingdom-ministry particularly well:

in relation to demonic oppression, conquest;
in relation to misrepresentation of God's rule, sharp rebuke;
in relation to selfish complacency, warning;
in relation to sin and failure, forgiveness and assurance of love;
in relation to sickness, healing;
in relation to material need, provision of daily bread;
in relation to exclusion, welcoming inclusion;
in relation to desire for power, an example of humble and loving service;
in relation to death, life;
in relation to false peace, painful division, but in relation to emnity, reconciliation.[10]

Jesus saw the kingdom of God as both *present* in a provisional way, in his ministry of mighty works and preaching,[11] and *future*, at the harvest of the world at the end of the age[12] when he as the Son of Man would come again in his glory[13] to establish the reign of God in fullness throughout the earth. But in both its present and future forms the kingdom was uniquely and crucially allied with himself. As he warned his critics among the Pharisees, to look for the (coming of) the kingdom of God apart from Jesus was to mistake it and miss it,[14] for the kingdom of God was there and then, 'among' them (NIV margin), in their midst. In Jesus, God had already come to inaugurate and work out his reign in grace: it was from the start, and would be until the final judgement, 'the acceptable year of the Lord'.[15] Already men and women were pressing into it and suffering for it.[16] It was a treasure within reach of all who heard its message[17] but one which would be taken away from an unbelieving nation and given to the Gentiles.[18] It was a feast to which all were invited, a seed growing secretly, a dragnet trawling the generations.[19]

Its fullness however lies in the future.[20] That future is today as ever the Church's goal and her inheritance.[21]

The kingdom in its fullness lies in the future: and in the future not as a human evolution but as a divine consummation.[22] It is a future in God and with God,[23] and it lies nowhere else. The politics of earth cannot substitute for, or even achieve, the kingdom of heaven. 'Utopia' is nowhere, but our life in the kingdom of God is 'wrapped up with Christ in God' (my translation of Colossians 3:4!) and is safe and sure. This future emphasis is needed lest we make claims which are unsubstantiable in the present 'age'. Here the kingdom has only come provisionally. Caesar, sin and sickness still hold great sway[24] but not to defeat the purposes of God. Here we too can claim much by faith, but because we live in the world of the Fall and share to some extent its fallen-ness still, we must reckon with Paul's words, 'your body is dead because of sin, yet your spirit is alive because of righteousness.'[25] This knowledge saves us from a foolish triumphalism such as the Corinthian believers fell into.[26]

The Christian and the Church thus live 'between the times': after the kingdom of God has come but before it has fully come. Our striking witness to the world has to be as a people who live the future in the present. Our church communities are to be outposts of that future world in this present world, communities of men and women who are struggling with all the realities of this life but who do so as children of the kingdom, journeying toward its glorious fullness with that light flickering on our faces and praying always: 'Your kingdom come'.

Notes

1 Mark 1:15.
2 Luke 4:16–19.
3 See David Bosch, *Transforming mission*, Maryknoll, Orbis Books, 1991, pp.110, 111, and I. H. Marshall, *The Gospel of Luke*, Exeter, Paternoster Press, 1978, pp. 185, 186.
4 Luke 4:24–30.
5 George Beasley-Murray, *Jesus and the Kingdom of God*, Exeter, Paternoster Press, 1986, p.227.
6 See e.g. Luke 11:20; 17:20–1.
7 Rev. 11:15.
8 Mark 10:45.
9 John 13:3–17.
10 Richard Bauckham, *The Bible in politics*, London, S.P.C.K., 1989, p.143.
11 Matt. 11:5–6; 12:28.
12 Matt. 13:24 ff.
13 Matt. 25:31 ff., cf. Dan. 7:13–14; Mark 14:62.
14 Luke 17:20–1.
15 Luke 4:19.
16 Matt. 11:12.
17 Matt. 13:44–6.
18 Matt. 21:43.
19 Matt. 22:1–14; Mark 4:26–9; Matt. 13:47–50.
20 Matt. 19:28–30.
21 Acts 14:22; 1 Cor. 15:50; 2 Tim. 4:1.
22 Matt. 25:31–4; Luke 19:11; 2 Tim. 4:1, 18.
23 Col. 3:1–3.
24 John 18:33, 36; 19:10–11; Acts 4:25–8; 2 Tim. 4:20.
25 Rom. 8:10.
26 1 Cor. 4:8–13; 2 Cor. 12:7–10.

THE COMMUNITY OF THE KINGDOM

Jesus not only preached the kingdom of God but estab-
lished its community in relation to himself. From the
beginning he gathered disciples who were both part of
this community and the means of its increase[1] and he
taught them in ways which distinguished them from the
world at large. So, in the Sermon on the Mount for
example, we have not a *prescription* for society in general but a *description* of the children of the kingdom
(the poor in spirit, the meek, the merciful, the pure in
heart etc.) with a corresponding series of directions for
their lives which can only flow from such people (e.g.
heart-obedience, spiritual worship, trust and fruitfulness).
It is true that some of the more famous illustrations of
the principles Jesus lays down (e.g. turning the other
cheek, giving to someone who wants to sue you for
your tunic your cloak as well) are not to be taken with
wooden literalism. They are 'mashals', that is vivid and
extreme sayings which were typically used in Israelite
teaching-style to make a serious point in a dramatic
and memorable way.[2] However, even the principles of
conduct set out in the Sermon on the Mount are not only
impracticable but quite impossible without the love and
power of God ruling the heart. That is why the Sermon
can never be used as a blueprint for society at large in its
secular state.

What Jesus is doing, there and elsewhere, is speaking
more to the Church than to the world: to God's kingdom
rather than Caesar's. For the Church is to be the community of the kingdom: belonging to its King, walking by
its laws, living in its powers and inheriting its future.
Although the kingdom in its fullness and universality is
still in the future, Christ has set that future irresistibly

in motion in the here-and-now, bringing its life to us and into us.

The Church is not the kingdom, but the Church is the *product* of the kingdom and the *channel* of the kingdom: an outpost in history of what will one day succeed history as we now see it in a fallen world. The Church is to be the sign of the future to the world: the sign of *God's* future. As Eddie Gibbs puts it, 'The Church is more than the herald announcing the message, it is a demonstration model which gives credence to the effectiveness of that message.'[3] So the Church is to exhibit the kingdom of God and the life of 'the age to come' in a life of reconciliation and peace, truth and justice, love and faith: touching the untouchables, including the excluded, out-facing the powers that keep people from God, modelling the life of the kingdom in our Church communities – the churches. These are to be communities of reconciled people in societies of alienated people; communities of caring people in a world of individuals too preoccupied to care; communities of love and peace, encouragement and strength, commitment and loyalty.

This is the life of the kingdom in the Church of God. Such a life may at present be only partially and imperfectly grasped and lived; it might appear weak and irrelevant to the world. But it was and is a mustard-seed beginning of a new and mighty future, a parable of what would be; leading us by small steps towards a great destiny – for the meek will inherit the earth at the coming of the King.

Jesus's message about the kingdom is essentially one of joy. He preached the good news of the kingdom, and the good news is that it is offered to 'the poor': the sinful, the failed, the excluded, the hopeless. It is to those who receive it 'like a little child' in the humility of faith[4] who discover its riches and its joy. It is the treasure hidden in a field, the pearl of great value, and those to whom it is offered are happy to pay any price for it.[5] The joy of receiving it is a joy shared by God himself: indeed it is *his* joy in us becoming one with our joy in him.[6]

68

The Church of God is to be a community of joy and celebration.

Have you noticed how often in the gospels we read about parties, banquets, feastings and merriment? Jesus seems to have attended more parties than funerals and very often uses the image of a banquet in his parables.[7] There is in fact serious theology involved in this!

The Jews looked forward to the 'Messianic banquet' in the age to come and Jesus used this imagery to express the joy of that age. Moreover his presence at celebrations private and public, usually with him at the centre, was a present, visible demonstration of it, indicating the critical truth that the long promised and awaited kingdom was even then present in Jesus's words and deeds. The most famous of his 'party parables' is that of the great banquet where those originally invited to a feast excused themselves in various ways and were replaced by 'the poor, the crippled, the blind and the lame'.[8] The point, not to say the sting, is well made by E. Linneman:

> The Pharisees do not believe that the kingdom of God is beginning *now* and see no connection between this event and Jesus' table fellowship with the lost. But Jesus places the situation in the light of a parable in which some people are not prepared to respect the fact that *the meal has already begun* and have to put up with the consequences. Anyone who is not willing to be summoned to the first course does not get to taste the meal proper.[9]

The deep seriousness of this is graphically expressed in various parables and sayings: in the dismay of the foolish virgins locked out of the wedding feast, in the confusion and shame of those who have no 'wedding garment' for the feast, and most starkly in the weeping, wailing and gnashing of teeth of those unable to enter the kingdom because they have rejected the King, while others rejoice to be in it because, for all their sin, they accepted him.[10]

When we pray 'Your kingdom come' we should realise

that we are praying about something very serious: we are praying about something which will be as terrible to some as it will be joyful to others. We are praying for the closing of the door as well as opening of the gates;[11] the final exclusion of the unbelieving, including the undecided,[12] as well as the entrance of a redeemed and reconciled race into its destiny, the kingdom prepared for it from the foundation of the world.[13] We are praying for the end of the old order with its space for repentance[14] as well as its pain and its tears;[15] we are praying for the new heaven and new earth[16] and for the final state of the city of God which will enfold nations but exclude the ungodly.[17] In a word, we pray, 'Come, Lord Jesus, come quickly, for salvation and judgement', whenever we pray 'Your kingdom come'.

Notes

1 Matt. 4:18–22.
2 e.g. Luke 14:26.
3 Eddie Gibbs, *I Believe in church growth*, London, Hodder & Stoughton, 1985, p. 142.
4 Luke 18:17.
5 Matt. 13:44–6.
6 Luke 15:7, 10, 23–4.
7 e.g. Matt. 8:11; 11:19; 22:1–14; 25:10; Mark 2:15–16, 19–20; 6:42–4; 8:8–9; 14:25; Luke 14:8; 8:12–14, 15–24; 15:1–2, 22–4; 19:5–10; John 2:1–10; 12:2; 21:9–13.
8 Matt. 22:1–14; Luke 14:16–24.
9 E. Linneman quoted in George Beasley-Murray, *Jesus and the Kingdom of God*, Exeter, Paternoster Press, 1986, p. 121.
10 Matt. 22:1–14; 25:1–13.
11 Matt. 25:10.
12 Matt. 25:46.
13 Matt. 25:34.

14 Rom. 2:5; 2 Pet. 3:9.
15 Rev. 21:4.
16 Rev. 21:1.
17 Rev. 21:6–8, 22–7; 22:14–15.

THE KINGDOM OF HEAVEN AND THE POLITICS OF EARTH

In his study of ethics in the Old Testament, Christopher J.H. Wright makes the following observation about God's deliverance of Israel from Pharaoh's Egypt:

> One outstanding feature of the redemption achieved at the exodus was its comprehensiveness. In that one sequence of events God gave to Israel a four-fold freedom: *politically* from the tyranny of a foreign autocratic power; *socially* from the intolerable interference in their family life; *economically* from the burden of enforced slave-labour; *spiritually* from the realm of foreign gods into the unhindered worship of the Lord and covenant relationship with him.[1]

It is true that we do not live our lives under the old covenant or in the Mosaic polity. Yet as the passage quoted above shows, it indicates what God hates in the world and shows how his activity in grace in any of its forms will work against the cruelties that disfigure human beings as societies and as individuals. Consequently the work of his kingdom should not be divorced from the world, which still stands outside it and it will never be irrelevant to that society. However, neither should it be submerged in that society, lost in or made redundant by societies' social programmes, developing ethics (where they do develop!) or democratic politics.

Here we encounter two extremes which Church history has witnessed among 'the children of the kingdom': withdrawal from the world and identification with the world; the abandonment of the state and surrender to the state; the failure to observe their civil duty on the one hand

and the failure to preserve their Christian identity on the other hand.

When Jesus prayed for his Church he asked God for protection but not isolation: 'My prayer is not that you take them out of the world but that you protect them from the evil one.'[2] When Jesus said to Pilate, 'My kingdom is not of this world . . . my kingdom is from another place,'[3] he certainly did not mean that his kingdom had nothing to do with this world. He meant his kingdom was not constructed from the materials of this world – its politics, its powers, its historical processes. It is of God and from God and comes from another world. However, it does come *into* this world (into what we in our vanity call 'the real world') and affects its people and its politics, its social order and its reforms.

As the children of the kingdom, the people of God are said by Jesus to be 'the salt of the earth' and 'the light of the world'. Both of these imply contact with our societies and both suggest that something is very wrong in those societies, needing our message and its demonstration. Salt, after all, was used as a preservative on dead carcasses not live animal, and the force of Jesus's metaphor suggests the spiritual death and tendency to decay which inevitably characterises society apart from God. There is a law of entropy, a tendency to break down, in fallen human nature and its organisations and institutions. The innate selfishness of the human heart and its capacity for cruel exploitation threaten all its institutions: marriages, work-relations, social services, good citizenship (think just of your tax returns!), political and international affairs. Only the universal grace of God preserves human society from its own evil, and God has ordained the people of his kingdom to show and to urge a better way.

However, we live in a world that has long rejected the kingship of God and frequently scorns the voice of his people. Human societies have set up a series of substitutes for his kingdom, culminating in the modern, secular state and its liberal democracy. We may well believe that in the democratic state the politics of this world have reached the peak of their evolution. But its problems have continued to multiply and its failures are clearly seen in our modern history and in our daily newspapers. The twentieth century saw the utter failure of Victorian optimism. The expected golden age produced not Tennyson's 'Parliament of man' but Stalin's gulags and Hitler's death-camps, war-casualties in scores of millions and a cold war between two superpowers with unimaginable potential for destruction.

Today, with world war behind us and nuclear war less likely, we are witnessing once more the rise of old nationalisms and tribalisms, distorted and poisoned by centuries-long hatreds. A multiplicity of small powers, as virulent and cruel as any superpower could ever be, is filling the political and military vacuums with human greed, prejudice and violence. As I write, twenty-five wars are taking place in various parts of the globe, creating huge suffering, and all the politics of man and the diplomacy of nations cannot bring peace to our world.

Even where there is no civil strife there is betrayal and breakdown in marriages; exploitation, injustice and alienation in the market-place; and growing crime and violence in our cities.

In the midst of this the kingdom of God is persistently at work, especially in and through the lives and witness of Christian men and women who are truly living by the principles of the kingdom and not the prejudices and preoccupations of the world. These are to be at one and the same time identified with the world and separate from it; identified with its needs and its problems but separate from its conspiracy to keep God out of its solutions! Hence, at one and the same time, we are the world's friends and its critics, we challenge as well as comfort, demolish as well as construct.[4] We must make the best of what is and work for what is not, and at the end of the day still cry, 'This is not enough!' We are to be occupied in this world but not preoccupied with it nor with our successes in it, short of the rescue of men and women to eternal salvation, 'for the form of this world is passing away'.[5] Hence the waiting Church, though she is always to be working as well as waiting, will still pray as she works for a better world: 'Your kingdom come'.

Notes

1 Christopher J.H. Wright, *Living as the people of God*, Leicester, IVP, 1985, p.74, my italics.
2 John 17:15.
3 John 18:36.
4 2 Cor. 10:4–5.
5 1 Cor. 7:29–31.

THE KINGDOM OF GOD AND THE MISSION OF THE CHURCH

A call to world mission is at the heart of Christianity. Even before the coming of Christ, it was central to God's plan[1] and to the prophetic vision[2] of the Old Testament. God is a missionary God, the Bible is a missionary book and Jesus called for a missionary Church. He said he was the light, not only of Israel, but of the world,[3] the good shepherd who had sheep far beyond that 'sheep-pen'.[4] He said he was the one who would drive out 'the prince of this world' and 'draw all men' to himself.[5] And his unique claims laid upon his followers a call to make him known to the world for which he died.[6]

From the start Jesus placed world mission near the top of the Church's agenda. At the start of his public ministry his call to Simon and Andrew, who were fishing in the Sea of Galilee, was 'Come, follow me and I will make you fishers of men,'[7] and before his ascension to heaven the same call was repeated as a commission, and indeed a command: 'All authority in heaven and on earth has been given to me. Therefore go and make disciples of all nations, baptising them in the name of the Father and of the Son and of the Holy Spirit.'[8]

This note is sounded similarly at the end of the other gospels[9] and Acts is to an extent the record of the apostolic obedience to it.[10] The mission of the early Church and its leaders issued not only from a Christ-given command but also from a Pentecostal experience of joy and power in the Holy Spirit.[11] The whole Church was involved in this expansion; it was spontaneous, natural and quite unstoppable. Leaders like Paul and Peter planted churches in the Middle East, Turkey and Europe. Yet they never thought to professionalise the Church's evangelism, but congratulated the young churches on their public and well-known witness.[12] The New Testament Church was self-consciously an evangelising Church and a missionary Church.

No one then could have foreseen twenty centuries of continuing world history with its space for repentance,[13] the advances and setbacks of Church history or a present-day Christian Church numbering believers in hundreds of millions. However, their astonished delight at our numbers would surely have been tempered in many places by dismay at our loss of vision, our worldliness and our sheer anonymity in the world.

In so many of our comfortable, affluent Western churches, world mission has indeed been 'the Church's withered arm'. There has been a failure to realise the plight of the lost and the potential of the saved. Our comparatively secure, trouble-free existence has led us into counting many blessings but not missed opportunities. Our building programmes far outstrip our mission strategies and our building funds dwarf our missionary giving. Many churches which support a missionary society never think of seriously praying that one of their own number may be sent, or of urging them to consider going with their church's full financial support and blessing. Yet few experiences more joyfully enlarge a church's vision and give them a taste of the Acts vision. Instead we confess, and even celebrate weekly, good news we do not tell, a commission we never think to take up, a claim for Christ we dare not make openly. Our enemies in this are as much within us as around us. We are embarrassed to witness openly, we would not dream of leaving promising careers and home comforts to take the message of Jesus to other nations and tribes, we even feel we have no right any longer to say or even think that people of other religions need to know the gospel of Jesus to be saved. But if Jesus is right they do! His apostles too lived in a pluralistic and religiously tolerant society, but they challenged its gods and changed the course of history with the spread of their proclamation of the truth that is in Jesus. Michael Green has renewed that challenge in these words:

> How can all religions lead to God when they are so different? . . . Christianity teaches that God both forgives a man and gives him supernatural aid. In Buddhism there is no forgiveness and no supernatural aid. The goal of all existence in Buddhism is *nirvana*, extinction – attained by the Buddha after no less than 547 births. The goal of all existence in Christianity is to know God and enjoy him for ever . . . Perhaps the greatest difference of all lies between the Bible which asserts that nobody can save himself and make himself pleasing to God, try as he will, and almost all the other faiths which assert that by keeping their teachings a man will be saved or re-born or made whole or achieve fulfilment . . . I just want to show how utterly illogical it is to say that they are all pointing in the same direction. It is as foolish as to say that all roads from Nottingham lead to London. They do nothing of the sort, and it is not helpful in the least to pretend that they do.[14]

As well as sending out long-term missionaries, one of the great joys of our own church here in Nottingham is to see students, post-graduates and others going out to South America, Africa, Europe and the Far East as short-term workers in a host of situations for medical, social and directly evangelistic work. Whether for a few months or one or two years, such an investment into God's work abroad can be of great value. Short-term workers are not to be despised. A short-term worker can end by becoming a long-term one! A short-term worker can give a long-term worker, or family, a much-needed vacation. A short-term worker can be used to train others in necessary skills from medicine to carpentry.

However, for every Christian the mission of the Church involves home mission. Even if you never set foot in another land your own mission-field lies around you.

You are crucially strategic to God's plans for the spread of his kingdom. There are people only you, of all other Christians, will meet, places only you will go, opportunities only you will have. Your circle, at work or in the extended family, may have no other opportunity to hear the good news of Jesus Christ clearly and personally. You may often experience rebuffs and discouragement, but you will also experience curiosity, openness, and a real desire to know God. You may be the only person they will ever talk to who knows God! Don't say, 'Oh, my testimony is very ordinary, very unimpressive, very dull.' That is, frankly, ludicrous. If God has stepped into your life then that is anything but dull to someone who has never known God. Just tell it as it is, without apology and with unashamed gratitude. We often fear we will not be able to argue our own case convincingly or answer the objections which are commonly raised against the Christian faith. Well, certainly, we Christians ought to study our faith in order to give good reason for the hope we have.[15] However, when our *life* demonstrates the love and righteousness of God we don't need to argue fiercely or to know all the answers. One of the best proofs of the gospel of Jesus Christ is the changed characters and lives of his followers. When your life is a light, people won't ask you if there *is* a light but where you got it from!

God in heaven has a kingdom on earth. We belong to that kingdom because we have been called by the King, Jesus who is Lord. That kingdom is a growing kingdom. It has grown through twenty centuries and it is growing in our own. Yet its expansion is through us and not apart from us, and through us as we are and not just as we would like to be. In his book *Know and tell the gospel*, John Chapman writes:

The hardest part of all evangelism is starting. We will do almost anything except begin. We do another training course, read another book. We form yet another committee and even go to a prayer meeting about it. But if you have not started – IT IS TIME. The best way to learn is to do it. None of us is much good at the beginning.[16]

Some pray for power (quite rightly)[17] but *do* nothing in their lives which requires it. God does not give power to waste: he gives power commensurate with the situation. One preacher I know illustrates this by referring to the National Grid. All the electric power is fed through that, but in use the power is stepped down by transformers. That's why you don't get millions of volts poured into your toaster! Even so, God gives power according to need, real need. You don't get a Pentecost to give someone a tract. You don't need it. But when you get into Pentecostal trouble for Christ, you'll get Pentecostal power from Christ.[18]

Keep a look-out during the day for its unique opportunities, its 'divine appointments', to help someone in the name of Christ, to bring the Lord Jesus one step nearer to someone's life, perhaps to be a link in a chain, a golden link in a golden chain, with others, to take Jesus to them, even at last to explain clearly the good news about 'the Saviour of the World'.[19] Each morning before the work of the day begins, pray 'Who today, Lord?', 'Where today, Lord?', 'How today, Lord?' Every day will be different but each day will have its possibilities and its significance. This is *your* part in the prayer 'Your kingdom come'; and it's unique!

Notes

1 Gen. 12:3.
2 Isa. 2:1–5.
3 John 8:12.
4 John 10:16.
5 John 12:32.
6 1 John 2:2.
7 Mark 1:17.
8 Matt. 28:18–19.

9 Mark 16:15; Luke 24:27; John 20:21.

10 Acts 1:8.

11 Acts 1:4–5; 2:1–11, 42–7; 4:29–31; 5:41–2; 8:4.

12 e.g. 1 Thess. 1:7–10.

13 2 Pet. 3:4,9.

14 Michael Green, *You must be joking*, London, Hodder & Stoughton, 1981, p. 43.

15 1 Pet. 3:15.

16 John Chapman, *Know and tell the gospel*, London, Hodder & Stoughton, 1981, p. 104.

17 Acts 1:4–5.

18 Acts 4:1–22, 30–1.

19 John 4:25.

21

YOUR WILL BE DONE ON EARTH!

It is of course a serious thing to pray that the whole world will be dominated by one will. Have we not seen terrible things done in totalitarian states where a particular ideology was imposed? Moreover, to many people it is an unwelcome and challenging thought that the individual's will should be subject to another's will. Does this mean that we should be unthinking, identikit creatures; mere items in a master-plan? Does it mean the end of independence and even integrity, the end of self-fulfilment and the pursuit of happiness?

If by independence we mean a life independent of God (that is, as far as we *can* live it!) then certainly this must end whenever God asserts his lordship and wherever his name is hallowed. But the end of that kind of independence does not mean the end of individuality and true freedom. Rather, in God we find our uniqueness and true freedom to be what he meant us to be. God's will does not crush us into anonymity and a mass with others; it develops, directs and guides us towards a full flowering of our God-intended beauty and usefulness in this world and the world to come. For God's will is not to be separated from his love, and what he wills for us will prove to be best for us. It is our wisdom to learn this.

I sometimes tell congregations the story of a large cargo of exotic South American birds which was being shipped to Europe many years ago for sale. During the voyage one of the birds got out of its cage. Efforts to recapture it in the hold only ended with it getting out to the deck and then escaping from the ship altogether. The sailors helplessly watched it fly triumphantly into the blue sky – free, free ('free as a bird' I suppose we might say!). They gave it up for lost and carried on with their tasks. However, a few days later the same bird reappeared and collapsed on deck, bedraggled and exhausted. It had discovered that there are not many trees in mid-Atlantic! It had been 'free' but found no rest; its freedom was fatal to its survival in a hostile environment.

So it is for human beings. We too take our flight into folly, insisting on our freedom to do our own thing and live without God thinking 'He is, after all, so restrictive.' But our freedom leaves us exhausted and threatened in a fallen world. Satisfaction eludes us, rest is denied us, and hostile forces, time and chance, and death at the end, wait to defeat us. We may live in rebellion against God, but our freedom is fatal: it is the freedom of the bird which was made for the rain forests trapped in mid-Atlantic; the freedom of the traveller lost in the wastes of a desert. For life without boundaries, without guidance, without God, becomes life without meaning or purpose or peace.

There is no prayer more right, more sure, more hopeful, than the prayer 'Your will be done' – for individuals and for societies. Men and women resent it, but we may ask what has opposition to God and his ways done for us in history and in the present? We have not gained by our stubbornness. The kingdoms of man have been failures and the self-worship of the individual is leading more and more to frustration, unhappiness and even cruelty.

Only the kingdom of God is 'righteousness and peace and joy in the Holy Spirit'. To know God is the end of despair; to become his child is the beginning of hope; to enter his kingdom is to enter an abundant life and to follow his will is the way of peace. We often read on the goods we buy: 'Follow the maker's instructions'. If we do not we should not be surprised to encounter breakdown and ruin of the best device. But our society, our race, has been resisting, contravening and modifying the Maker's instructions since the Fall, and we have not proved cleverer or wiser than God. Someone has said, 'History is a series of breakdowns on the road of progress.' And none of our politics or philosophies or social sciences have been able to free us from our trouble.

Why? Because we ourselves are our worst enemies. Our trouble is in our own hearts, not our systems. And so it will continue to be as long as we say to God not 'Your will be done' but 'My will be done' or 'Our will be done.' Collectively and individually we are, in and of ourselves, hopelessly flawed. Only God, the God of hope, can rescue and remake us. The God whose will is done in heaven is the God whose will must be done on earth if earth is ever to be happy and men and women brought to fulfilment. So the Church prays for herself and for the world, 'Your will be done on earth as it is in heaven.'

22

THE CALL TO DISCIPLESHIP

God's will must be done 'on earth' not only generally but in our own hearts and lives in particular. And in a fallen world where human wills are so commonly opposed to God's will, the surrender of our wills to his is a significant and even dramatic event each and every time we do it. Each time we say, with sincerity and meaning, 'Your will be done' we are bringing both the past and the future into the present. We are re-living that surrender to God which marked our first entrance into his kingdom and we are bringing the future, when God's will shall be done throughout the earth, into the present. In that place, at that precise moment of prayer, the kingdom has come a little more and the end is a little nearer.

Yet it is not without resistance that the rule of the King extends itself into every part of our lives. We find it easy enough to say 'Your will be done' until that will clashes with ours, challenges ours, denies ours and conquers ours. We are not used to having our will thwarted or our rights questioned. We were told that life is at our feet and now we must learn to lay it at God's feet. We were told that we must 'go out there and make it happen', imposing our will on a situation, and now we must repeatedly yield up our will to God's will. This is not only a new way of thinking, it is also a new way of living, of acting and reacting, of planning and scrapping our plans. It takes a lot of will-power to surrender our will; it needs the grace of God to yield to God's grace; but we only conquer when we surrender:

> My will is not my own
> Till Thou hast made it Thine;
> If it would reach a Monarch's throne

It must its crown resign:
It only stands unbent,
Amid the clashing strife,
When on Thy bosom it has lent,
And found in Thee its life.[1]

The call of Jesus is and always has been to discipleship.
The Greek word for disciple is *mathetes* which really
means 'learner'. In the first-century world of the gospels,
every rabbi had his pupils, his learners, his disciples. They
submitted to his teaching, to his 'yoke' as the saying went
(hence Jesus's words, 'Take my yoke upon you and learn
of me').[2] Against that background, a disciple was firstly
one who surrendered his judgement to his rabbi. That was
where all true discipleship had to start: learning from the
teacher. In our case, we can learn from the best and wisest
teacher that ever lived, who knew God his Father as no
other knew or could know him[3] and whose life was the
perfect commentary on his teaching.[4] However, we cannot
stop at that.

Our first duty as disciples of Christ is not only to listen
to him and to learn from him but also to believe in him.
When his critics asked Jesus, 'What must we do to do the
work God requires?', he answered, 'The work of God is
this: to believe in the one he has sent.'[5] Jesus called for
faith and permanent self-giving. For Jesus is not among
those teachers who talk and only require listeners, or
those who philosophise and only produce theorists. He
calls us to follow him as Lord and Master, his willing
servants, his faithful friends. Doing God's will is the end
and sign of all true religion.[6] As we are not to be hearers
only,[7] so we are not to be pray-ers only. Liturgy without
life-style, the form of religion without the power and the
practice of it, is everywhere in the Bible condemned as
worthless.[8] The call of Christ is to faith and works, that is,
to the faith *which* works. He calls us to serve our brothers
and sisters,[9] to bear fruit in love and good works[10] and so
demonstrate ourselves to be disciples indeed.[11] Someone
has said, 'Jesus calls us down from the balcony where we

are applauding him to the dusty road where we must follow him.' And when we find ourselves weary, uncomfortable and rejected, we must ask, not 'Is it worth it?', but 'Is *he* worth it?'

> All I once held dear, built my life upon,
> All this world reveres and wars to own,
> All I once thought gain I have counted loss;
> Spent and worthless now, compared to this.
>
> Knowing you, Jesus, knowing you,
> There is no greater thing.
> You're my all, you're the best,
> You're my joy, my righteousness,
> And I love you, Lord.[12]

Notes

1 'Make me a captive, Lord', George Matheson (1842–1906).
2 Matt. 11:29.
3 Matt. 11:27.
4 Matt. 11:30.
5 John 6:28–9.
6 Matt. 7:21–3.
7 Jas. 1:22.
8 e.g. Isa. 1:10–17; Jas. 2:14–26.
9 John 13:12–17.
10 Matt. 5:14–16; John 15:8.
11 1 John 3:14; 5:2.
12 'All I once held dear', Graham Kendrick, Croydon, Make Way Music, 1993.

23

NEED AND OBEDIENCE

We live in an increasingly need-based society where our 'needs', or what we think we need or what we are told we need, are the centre-point and the determining factor of personal morality and national economies. This has led to some unforeseen but not unforeseeable results. Our needs have grown steadily, our expectations have become unrealistic and our feelings of disappointment have in many cases become savage. Our needs have become our rights, and if they are withheld we are presumed to have suffered injustice. We ourselves imagine ourselves to have been reduced if our needs remain unmet. The effect of this has been startling and disturbing and far from our expectations. We are reduced by that very process which believes that we are only the sum of our needs and that the purpose of life is only to supply those needs. The meeting of needs becomes the process by which we become fully human. In his book *All you love is need*, Tony Walter suggests that we have moved from Descartes' 'I think therefore I am' to 'I need therefore I am.'[1] These needs have become our starting point and our finishing point: you are what you eat/drive/wear/project. In this view 'personality development is nothing but the meeting of personal needs, the economy is nothing but the meeting (or exploiting) of needs, marriage is nothing but the meeting of needs . . . Need is the religion of the religionless, the morality of those who have progressed beyond morality.'[2]

The startling contrast with this thinking which is presented by Christianity is illustrated most powerfully by Jesus Christ himself:

The Christian faith is founded on a man whom Christians believe to be the most complete person this world has ever known. By present standards this man was poor in material things. He was not married, had no children and gave up his job in order to become an itinerant and unpaid preacher. The totalitarian Roman Empire in which he lived denied him many of those things which today are regarded as basic human needs. Moreover Jesus taught that far from basing our life on the needs of the self, we should take up our cross and deny our self.[3]

This does not mean, however, that human needs are irrelevant or that human beings are only to be assessed in 'spiritual' or non-material terms. Poverty *is* degrading and harmful, sickness and death are the enemy of us all, there are human rights as well as human wrongs. The harm is done when the supplying of every felt need becomes central and dominant, when the supplying of needs which are not in fact essential to human existence becomes the main reason for human existence, when rights are not balanced with responsibilities to others and become duty-less rights in a selfish and increasingly hedonistic society. It is from these things that our own affluent Western society is suffering.

And it is from such things that we in the Church are suffering, too! There is a great craving in this post-modern age for a religion which will fulfil us but not restrain us, which will give us all we lack but not take from us anything we want; which will leave our sin unchallenged and our conscience padded with comfort. We speak of 'hurts' more than sins and present Jesus as the One people need if they are to be truly happy and fulfilled. Thomas A. Smail in *The forgotten Father* has some salutary corrections to make in this regard:

There is no doubt at all that for all of us much of the time it is our need that sets us running in a God-ward direction and God's grace consists precisely in the fact that he is ready to receive and deal with us on the basis of our need to supply it. But the purpose of

Jesus is never just to meet people's needs, it is always when they come with their needs to make disciples, to attach people to himself so that they no longer want for themselves, but want to follow him more than they want anything for themselves . . . There has been a conversion from a need-based relationship to Jesus to an obedience-based relationship.[4]

This is the fundamental shift which conversion accomplishes in the heart and lives of believers. The centrality of my needs gives way to the centrality of his honour, his glory, his will. We move from 'My will be done' to 'Your will be done'. This, however, is a process which needs to be affirmed and repeated daily in our lives as we say 'Your will be done', not only in our world at large but in our lives in particular. This process runs counter to so much of our old thinking and life-style that a true surrender, not without struggle, has to be renewed repeatedly in our inner and outer lives:

I was not ever thus, nor prayed that Thou
Shouldst lead me on;
I lived to choose and see my path; but now
Lead Thou me on.
I loved the garish day, and, spite of fears,
Pride ruled my will: remember not past years.[5]

These lives of ours are to show the world what happens when God's will *is* done 'on earth as it is in heaven' in our marriages, in our working lives and in our church communities, and in the lives of those we help in God's love and Jesus' name. Church communities should be working models of God's kingdom come among men and women, demonstrations of the future when the kingdom of God will be fully come and God will be all in all. Our churches are to be caring communities in a world too preoccupied, too suspicious or too defensive to care; communities rich and overflowing with love in a world short on love; communities which stimulate and develop faith in a world which devalues and discourages it; communities defined by Christ, headed by Christ and modelled on Christ; communities of true believers, who not only say in liturgy, 'Lord, Lord,' but do in life the will of our Father who is in heaven.[6]

Notes

1 Tony Walter, *All you love is need*, London, S.P.C.K., 1985, p. 154.
2 Tony Walter, p. 125.
3 Tony Walter, p. xiii.
4 Thomas A. Smail, *The Forgotten Father*, London, Hodder & Stoughton, 1987, pp. 163–4.
5 'Lead Kindly Light', J.H. Newman (1801–90).
6 Matt. 7:21.

'YOUR WILL BE DONE': THE KEYNOTE OF JESUS'S LIFE

More than any other figure in human history, Jesus Christ lived to fulfil the will of God his Father. That will was the map and mainspring of his life.

The writer to the Hebrews captures the spirit in which Christ came into the world by using and quoting from one of the Psalms: 'Then I said, "Here I am – it is written about me in the scroll – I have come to do your will, O God."'[1]

His coming into the world was an act of willing obedience, though it would cost him dear, as it cost the Father who 'so loved the world that he gave' – to Bethlehem and to Calvary – this Son who 'made himself nothing, taking the very nature of a servant'.[2] It was in servant-form that he could say: 'I have come down from heaven not to do my will but to do the will of him who sent me'[3] and 'I always do what pleases him'.[4] In *Christianity – the true humanism*, Thomas Howard and J. I. Packer note the character of this obedience in Jesus's life as freedom rather than restriction: 'Far from its having been a matter of "knuckling under" to some tyrannical father-figure, Jesus said that his very "meat" was to do his Father's will. In other words, he *enjoyed* his obedience: it was food and drink to him; it brought him strength and contentment; it left him satisfied.'[5]

The heartbeat of Jesus's obedience to the Father's will was love, and that love flowed out to those around him in all their diversity and need: to the crowds who were as sheep without a shepherd, to the sick and the bereaved, to children and disciples (the latter sometimes being another kind of children) and to his enemies, even those who crucified him. Love was his life, love his legacy and love his rule.[6]

From the life that loves issues the life that lives the prayer 'Your will be done'. That is the only possibility for authentic human existence:

> Now the rule or pattern, for our human life and hence for human freedom, says Christianity, is the rule of love. This is the will of God who called us into being. The point is, God is love and we are made in his image; which means, we have been made to live as he lives, doing at our level what he does at his. There is the axis of the whole pattern. We don't really know just how all the other creatures in the universe find their fulfilment, if we may speak thus. They seem to glorify God by simply being themselves – stars, waves, winds, dragonflies, snowflakes. But for us the stakes are higher. We are made like God, we are told, and we can find our fulfilment and joy only by loving as he loves, thus becoming increasingly like him in personal moral practice. There is no contentment and therefore no freedom for human creatures if we try to live any other way.[7]

Beyond every other act of obedience in that life which lived to obey the Father who sent him was Jesus's obedience 'unto death – even death on a cross!'.[8] Here at the threshold of hell, of desolation and the curse,[9] in full knowledge of the horrors in the cup he was given to drink, Jesus surrendered the last of his rights – the right to his Father's face: 'Father, if you are willing, take this cup from me; yet not my will, but yours be done.'[10]

The will of God may be expected to lead to heaven – but not to hell. Yet the Lord of glory becomes the outlaw and crosses over the border-line of all comfort into the desolation and anguish of hell, where there is no comfort. And he goes because it is his Father's will. He was the sinless Son, innocent of offence, 'Yet it was the Lord's will to crush him and cause him to suffer.'[11]

Why? Has God become vindictive, shall the judge of all the earth do wrong?

> But he was pierced for our transgressions, he was crushed for our iniquities; the punishment that bought us peace was upon him, and by his wounds we are healed. We all, like sheep, have gone astray, each of us has turned to his own way; and the Lord has laid on him the iniquity of us all.[12]

It was thus that the Christ fulfilled the 'must' of prophecy[13] under which he had consciously lived his whole life.[14] His final act of obedience was of a piece with the rest of his life, yet it was also the final and chief reason for his coming into the world. Yet though it was 'the Lord's will to crush him', 'it was impossible for death to keep its hold on him.'[15] He was led to the grave, but he was not left there. After the finished work, the full reward: the end of sufferings is the beginning of conquests,[16] '. . . and though the Lord makes his life a guilt offering, he will see his offspring and prolong his days, and the will of the Lord will prosper in his hand.'[17] The will of God which crushed him on earth carried him to heaven, the risen, exalted Son, victorious over sin and death and hell: 'Therefore God exalted him to the highest place and gave him the name that is above every name.'[18]

In all this there are depths we will never fathom, heights we will never scale – of humiliation and glory. Yet in all this too there are aspects we can imitate and elements we are called upon to share, both in Christ's sufferings[19] and in his glory:[20] 'I want to know Christ and the power of his resurrection and the fellowship of his sufferings, becoming like him in his death, and so, somehow, to attain to the resurrection from the dead.'[21]

Notes

1 Heb. 10:7.

2 John 3:16 with Phil. 2:7.
3 John 6:38.
4 John 8:29.
5 J.I. Packer and Thomas Howard, *Christianity: the true humanism*, Berkhamstead, Word Publishing, 1985, p. 63.
6 John 15:9–12; Matt. 5:44.
7 Packer and Howard, pp. 66–7.
8 Phil. 2:8.
9 Matt. 27:45; Gal. 3:13.
10 Luke 22:42.
11 Isa. 53:10.
12 Isa. 53:5–6.
13 Luke 22:37; 24:25–7, 44.
14 Luke 2:49; 4:43; John 9:4.
15 Acts 2:24.
16 John 12:32.
17 Isa. 53:10.
18 Phil. 2:9.
19 John 12:23–5; 15:12–14; Eph. 5:1–2; 1 Pet. 2:21.
20 Rom. 8:18–19; 1 Pet. 4:12–14; 5:4, 6; Rev. 2:10.
21 Phil. 3:10–11.

YOUR WILL BE DONE ON EARTH AS IT IS IN HEAVEN

A prayer like this can be understood in a number of ways.

Sometimes in Scripture God's 'will' is his eternal purpose, encompassing his decree and intentions which are sure to come to pass because he is the omnipotent God.[1] Thus his 'will' most certainly will be done in the end, both in heaven and on earth.[2] That is why the Old Testament could predict with confidence the coming of God and his kingdom even to a hostile and unpromising world, and the final triumph of good over evil. God was sovereign and his kingdom would triumph in 'the day of the Lord'. That too is why the New Testament can look forward with confidence to the triumph of Christ, at his second coming, when he will set up the kingdom of heaven on a renewed earth, filling it with his goodness and his glory. We should never underestimate or understate the sovereignty of God. It is essential to his 'God-ness' and to our happiness. Christian 'hope', in biblical language, is an expectation of a certain event, but with a God who was not sovereign it would soon dwindle to the level of hope commonly associated with the weather during next year's holidays.

Sometimes God's 'will' is his rule in a more present and direct way; his authority directing and controlling, his purposes coming to fruition in the present, his voice being heard among his people, his Church joyfully recognising that he is enthroned in its midst, even in the old order of things. At such times God's will demonstrates openly, sometimes marvellously, the presence of the kingdom, as when Peter and John say to the cripple who asked for money: 'Silver or gold I do not have, but what I have I give you. In the name of Jesus Christ of Nazareth, walk.'[3] This rule is, as we can see, disputed and opposed in the world; it is, like the kingdom, only partially and provisionally here; but it is prophetically demonstrated in the life of the Church where God's authority is recognised and his rule accepted.

Sometimes God's will is his grieving permission that we should share in the world's lot of suffering and loss. His ways do often lead through hard places in life. The problems around this are as old as the book of Job and as new as our own trials.

Sometimes for the Christian believer struggling through a world of evil and sorrow and pain, it is a prayer that has to be said in dark times when, as Jesus faced with the cross, we have to trust that God's will for us is best even when it means personal loss and suffering and even death.

God's way to our Easter morning often lies through a personal Gethsemane and beyond. At such times this is a prayer baptised in tears – tears that God knows and counts and shares. But he sees beyond the darkness and knows the plans he has for us[4] beyond the dark clouds and in the glory. So it was with Christ who, for the joy that was set before him, endured the cross.[5]

When we pray this prayer for ourselves as individuals, God's will is the guidance we seek for our own lives, as we pray for his wisdom and learn something of his plan for our lives, our careers, marriage, homes. The way forward may be uncertain in a matter which is perhaps very important for us. How can we obtain the guidance of God to do his will? We need to pray, to look for principles of conduct in God's word, to seek council from experienced and godly people. Yet even then we may be still unsure. Then it is that we must rest in the sovereignty of God as we tentatively move forward with this prayer still in our hearts. He is well able to recover the situation if we have made a wrong judgement, or to bring unexpected good out of our situation as things develop.

Our greatest duty is to seek his will in sincerity and self-giving, to trust his wisdom and love and to obey his word; and to leave the rest to a Father's care and kindness.

What is of most importance is not that we do not know God's will in a situation or decision, but that we are *seeking* to know and do God's will in that particular matter.

It is there we see what God has done in our lives already. We have been freed from the tyranny of 'I did it my way', released from the bondage of 'my will be done', cured of the compulsion of 'me first'. Yes, I know we can still be selfish and foolish and uncaring and there are disciplines yet to be acquired and desires yet to be conquered. But deep within our hearts is the cry, 'Father, Thy will be done', 'Lord take me, master me, make me all you want me to be.'

> Breathe on me, breath of God,
> Fill me with life anew,
> That I may love what thou dost love
> And do what thou wouldst do.
>
> Breathe on me, breath of God,
> Until my heart is pure;
> *Until my will is one with thine*
> To do and to endure.[6]

We long to say with Christ our Lord: 'I seek not my own will but the will of him who sent me.'[7] And we long too to see that will done throughout the earth. Hence we cry

Thy Kingdom come, O God,
The rule, O Christ, begin;
Break with thine iron rod
The tyrannies of sin.[8]

The Bible ends with precisely this vision.[9] This and this only is the hope of the world, the hope of men and women.

Notes

1 Isa. 46:9–10.

2 Acts 2:23; 4:28; Eph. 1:11.
3 Acts 3:6.
4 Jer. 20:10–11.
5 Heb. 12:2.
6 'Breathe on me, breath of God', Edwin Hatch (1835–1889).
7 John 5:30.
8 'Thy kingdom come, O God', Lewis Hensley (1824–1905).
9 Rev. 21:1–5, 22–7; 22:1–5.

III. GIVE US TODAY OUR DAILY BREAD

26

A LESSON IN PRIORITIES

These words hardly strike us as dramatic, but they surely
are. In one breath we speak of 'our heavenly Father',
and in the next 'our daily bread'; one moment it is 'your
will' and in the next 'my food'. We move in the same
solemn, exalted prayer from 'infinities and immensities'
to the weekly shop and the loaf on the table! Here are
lessons about God and about us: lessons in his care and
competence and lessons in our dependence and trust.
He does not forget our humanity; we must not forget
his divinity. He is a caring Father; we must be grateful
children.

The place of this petition in the whole prayer is significant in more than one respect: it gives us first of all a
lesson in priorities. Notice that it does not *begin* the Lord's
Prayer. The prayer begins with God's glory and only later
deals with our needs. It is most definitely 'Hallowed be
your name' before it is 'Give us our daily bread'. We are
taught in this way, by Christ, the priorities of prayer. We
so easily and so often begin with ourselves when we should
begin with God. We bring shopping lists to the Throne
as if God were a grocer, as if he existed for us and not
we for him. But 'Man's chief end [purpose] is to glorify
God and to enjoy him for ever'.[1] We displace much of
that enjoyment of God with the demands of life. We say
'Give us this' and 'Give us that' and 'Give us the other'
until we are prayed out, and there is no room for 'Give
us yourself' above all and, if it must be, instead of all:

> Thou, O Christ, art all I want;
> More than all in Thee I find[2]

Yes, God does answer our prayers. But how can we expect

answers to prayers we do not pray? Is our problem that God does give us what we ask for but not what we do *not* ask for? If that is often the case, then it is not surprising that so many Christians in our materialistic society are materially affluent but spiritually impoverished. We have what we want most – bread but not blessing! Is it surprising that God should hesitate to give us what we do not sufficiently value? And can we say we greatly value what we leave to the end of the list? We make sure we are well stocked-up each week from Sainsbury's or Tesco's, but live on iron rations when it comes to spiritual food obtained from prayer and the study of the Scriptures. Jesus too needed 'daily bread', but as to supreme priorities he could say firmly, 'My food is to do the will of God.'[3]

Our Lord Jesus tells us that not bread but *God* is 'the one thing necessary'.[4] Whatever else may be convenient and reasonable is also dispensable to a high degree – but not the hallowing of God's name known and loved as 'Father'. To possess not only bread but the farms that supply it, and the factories that bake it, and the outlet stores that retail it, and the millions that customers pay for it, but not to have the Giver who gave it, is to be poor while rich and empty while full; it is to live on the scraps of the divine life, missing its wholeness and its bounty, its dignity and its security.

It is true that we have all, at some time, burst into the presence of God in great fear or urgent need, and it is the measure of his fatherly love and understanding that he does not cast us back but embraces us and tenderly comforts us. Yet while even the Psalmist does this,[5] comfort does not come with real and lasting effect until he realises what *God* is and dwells on that for a while in praise and love, and *then* comes to his problem.

Always remember that God is more important than your troubles, and insist on giving him the place in all your prayers that he has in all the universe. The effect of this will not be to diminish you or your needs but it may well be to diminish your fears. It is when we begin with God in prayer that we get other things in perspective. Our immediate needs and fears retire to their right place. We begin to see the situation more clearly: our fears dwindle before God's all-sufficiency; our anxieties subside with the storm when Jesus stands up in the boat.[6] We are no longer lost in the crowd of events, because with the recognition of who God is there comes too the recollection of who we are. Then we can bring the problem to him and lay our needs before him, not in panic, but in reverence and quiet trust; then we can rise up and face the situation as we ought: whether the larder is empty or full.

The fact is that God must come before *everything* in our lives, before reputation,[7] before family loyalties,[8] before possessions[9] and even before life.[10] But when he is given his rightful and supreme place before and above all these things – then he does an astonishing and wonderful thing: he takes us up with himself, sits us alongside himself as his beloved children,[11] gives to us the kingdom,[12] shares with us the glory[13] and, whether we gain or lose in life's unequal market-place, he makes us more than conquerors through Christ who loved us.[14] He makes our concerns his concerns, our needs his care, our fragile lives the focus of his sovereign providence.

Notes

1 The Westminster Shorter Catechism, 1648, Question 1.
2 'Jesus, lover of my Soul', Charles Wesley (1707–88).
3 John 4:34.
4 Luke 10:42.
5 e.g. Ps. 71, 73, 77.
6 Mark 4:39.
7 Acts 5:41.
8 Matt. 10:37.
9 Heb. 10:34.
10 Rev. 12:11.

11 Eph. 2:6.
12 Luke 22:29.
13 John 17:24.
14 Rom. 8:37–8.

AN ANTIDOTE TO ANXIETY

Our Father in heaven is a Father who cares: about things small and great, temporal and eternal, physical and spiritual. The world of Jesus' day had as many agonies and uncertainties as the world of our day:

> The standard wage for a labourer in Jesus' day was a silver denarius a day. This was barely enough to keep a small family at subsistence level. If such a labourer did not find work for several days, his family was destitute. In such circumstances the fourth petition in the Lord's Prayer ('Give us today our bread for this day') takes on a poignancy many of us no longer experience. It is a prayer for survival.[1]

Yet Jesus, in the Sermon on the Mount, urges his followers not to be consumed with anxiety: 'Therefore I tell you, do not worry about your life, what you will eat or drink; or about your body, what you will wear.'[2] And he bases our peace on a relationship with a heavenly Father who knows and cares: one who feeds 'the birds of the air' and clothes 'the lilies of the field' and values his children who have much greater significance and a much more glorious destiny[3] than birds or flowers. To be obsessed with material as opposed to spiritual necessities is to live like those who acknowledge no heavenly Father.[4] It is to reverse the priorities of the kingdom: 'But seek first his kingdom and his righteousness, and all these things will be given to you as well.'[5]

Yet we immediately have a problem with such promises – and it is in part a very modern problem. We, in our time, have been encouraged to challenge everything, always to look for the exception, always to stress the negative.

We have made cynicism a virtue. The Psalmist could say, 'I was young and now I am old, yet I have never seen the righteous forsaken or their children begging bread.'[6] We could show him a thing or two! Give us the streets of Calcutta or Mexico City, a video camera and a time-machine, and we'll fill the gaps in his experience! But this is to miss his point. He too lives in 'the real world'. But he has learned to count blessings as well as ironies, to see the positive as well as the negative, and to see (as often those believers who have lived through hard times have seen) that while we are not immune to the tragedies and inequities of life in a fallen world, yet we are not alone in that world nor abandoned to it. Soon the Psalmist's spiritual descendants would learn of a God whose Son became a refugee at the beginning of his earthly life and a crucified victim of injustice at its end. Did God not care *then*? Was he uninvolved *there*?

We too sometimes fall victims to life's violence, tragedy and unfairnesses. Nevertheless, for most of us most of the time, the famous words of Psalm 91 are true: not as blank cheques but as day-passes through the dangers of life: 'He [she] who dwells in the shelter of the Most High will rest in the shadow of the Almighty . . . If you make the Most High your dwelling – even the Lord, who is my refuge – then no harm will befall you, no disaster will come near your tent.'[7]

And when it does, when the evil day comes: when the sparrow falls out of the nest[8] and evil slays the good,[9] the sacred sovereignty of God is still at work. Our Father knows the hairs of your head are all numbered;[10] we are not abandoned, our worth is not diminished.[11]

Here is a lesson in trust and an invitation to peace: even in the midst of dangers and in the process of struggle. The apostle Paul urges us to learn this lesson when he writes: 'Do not be anxious about anything, but in everything, by prayer and petition, with thanksgiving, present your requests to God. And the peace of God, which transcends all understanding, will guard your hearts and your minds in Christ Jesus.'[12]

108

Sometimes anxiety can be a kind of atheism. Our fears or problems fill the horizon until God is given no place; our worries are everywhere and God is nowhere. But he calls us to prayer: not to an escape from everything but to prayer 'in everything'. Prayer is not escapism, it is a unique kind of involvement. Our engagement with life as it is does not change but we who engage with it are changed. We are still occupied with our problems but no longer obsessed with them: prayer precedes our daily conflict, peace remains in that conflict at deep levels and at night we can, in thanksgiving, remember our Father's involvement and transcendence, his concern and his sovereignty, his deliverances in the past and his promises about the future.

A poem by Ulrich Schaffer on the fear and anxiety which threaten the believer at times ends with three lines that for me memorably capture our safety in the hands of our Father in heaven.

> Be my captain and my boat
> My oars and my sail
> And the water into which I fall.[13]

Notes

1 David Bosch, *Transforming mission*, Maryknoll, Orbis Books, 1991, p. 27.
2 Matt. 6:25.
3 Matt. 6:30.
4 Matt. 6:32.
5 Matt. 6:33.
6 Ps. 37:25.
7 Ps. 91:1, 9–10.
8 Matt. 10:29.
9 Matt. 10:28.
10 Matt. 10:30.

11 Matt. 10:31.
12 Phil. 4:6–7.
13 Ulrich Schaffer, *Into your light*, Leicester, IVP, 1979, p.46.

THE PROVIDENCE OF GOD

God's providence is in large measure his 'provide-ence', as the English word suggests. He is indeed the God who provides. In the Psalmist's words:

> The Lord is faithful to all his promises
> and loving towards all he has made.
> The Lord upholds all those who fall
> and lifts up all who are bowed down.
> The eyes of all look to you,
> and you give them their food at the proper time.
> You open your hand
> and satisfy the desires of every living thing.[1]

In the famous words of our Lord Jesus, God our heavenly Father feeds the birds, dresses the lilies and clothes the grass of the field.[2] This is not a blind romanticism. Jesus recognises the trouble of life[3] and its effects, but he recognises too the ineradicable and constant work of God sustaining a damaged earth: its ecology and its humanity. And of course, as we have seen, he recognises God's special concern for his own children, the children of the kingdom, the ones who daily pray this prayer because they have a relationship with God the provider, as their Father in heaven.

The provision prayed for here takes place precisely in a world of uncertainty, of inequity and of spoilation; of failed crops, of famine and of war. The Psalmist and his Lord both live in the same world as we do. But they do not blame God for its ills. Ours is a world which is not simply the world God made; it is also one which we have made. It is a world where there is food enough for all but where war has despoiled huge tracts of fertile land, where greed has over-exploited natural resources and where selfishness has unfairly distributed God's provision. Our world and its history are marked by the failure of human beings, not of God: 'The fault, dear Brutus, is not in our stars, but in ourselves.'[4] But it is also a world marked by the sovereign providence of God.

The Bible never allows us to relinquish our hold on the sovereignty of God. From first to last, God is sovereign. He created the world in its beginning, he will redeem it in the end and he overrules it in the meantime.[5]

There are great mysteries here, to be sure, the mystery of providence being one of the greatest. How can God be sovereign over a world which sidelines his existence, flouts his laws and violates his will? How can God be sovereign and human beings be free and responsible agents? We can see how a god can be good and not all-powerful, so that evil becomes, as in so many old religions and philosophies, an equal and opposite 'force' to good. We can see how a god can be all-powerful but not all good, having, as in some other dualistic systems, a dark as well as a light side. But to reconcile the God of the Bible with the world of the newspapers – that is hard: 'God Almighty and ills unlimited'; a God altogether good who does not prevent things altogether bad in our world, which is also his. A God who gives daily bread to millions in a world where millions more go undernourished or many starve to death.

We cannot make sense of all this – and neither does the Bible. Nor does it try! Indeed it is a question whether we can make 'sense' of sin which is nonsense, contrary to God's order, to life's truth and to our good. Sin has brought chaos to our world; our racial Fall brought 'death into the world, and all our woe', as Milton put it in *Paradise Lost*. But though sin brought many evils into the world, it did not expel God from the world! The God who cast Adam and Eve out of the Garden also went with them out of the Garden. The God who devastated the world in Noah's day also began a new chapter in salvation history in Abraham's day. The God who cursed the earth because of human sin[6] also entered that world 'in the likeness of sinful flesh' and bore its curse in himself, that those condemned might be forgiven and justified and become heirs of God's future for the world we spoiled.[7] The same God now, as ever, works increasingly in love and pain in this sinful world to call men and women to himself in repentance and faith.[8] God is almighty, but the ills of a fallen world are not unlimited. There will come a day when there will be 'no more death or mourning or crying' for the old, fallen, spoiled order of things will have passed away.[9]

Holy Scripture therefore faces *both* realities: God's goodness *and* mankind's cruelties, God's justice *and* life's inequalities, God's righteousness *and* our unrighteousness. It does not cover up sin, even in the best of its characters; and it does not compromise the righteousness of God, even in the worst of their sufferings.

We often hear of Auschwitz in this regard, and the terrible holocaust of the last war, as if there could no longer be talk of providence or omnipotence or even God. You would sometimes think God had built Auschwitz instead of suffering in its horrors! Israel in Isaiah's day and Judah in Jeremiah's day also had their holocaust; yet the prophets stood firm in the midst of all their tears and heartbreak.[10] And so must we.

More crucially still, the worst deed in all of human history, the crucifixion of the Son of God, was said to have taken place under God's sovereignty and not at the cost of it. On the day of Pentecost the apostle Peter preaches to the crowd about Jesus: 'This man was handed over to you by God's set purpose and foreknowledge; and you, with the help of wicked men, put him to death by nailing him to the cross.'[11] Here was an act of inexcusable human wickedness ('You . . . put him to death') which was ordained by God 'by God's set purpose'[12] and prefigures in Old Testament sacrifices and prophecies.[13] How, in this or in any subsequent event, God can seriously yet sinlessly ordain and overrule the free acts of human beings is a mystery beyond philosophy and beyond our little logic. But the writers of Scripture hold fast to the goodness and sovereignty of God[14] and to the culpability of a rebellious race and wicked people in it. He who gave them life will judge them in the end, and as his forgiveness now is mighty so his wrath then will be terrible.

Meantime, his people rely on his sovereignty for their confidence that he will triumph in the end,[15] that his kingdom will come and that the earth will in that day 'be filled with the knowledge of the glory of the Lord, as the waters cover the sea'.[16] We have his word for it!

Equally, that sovereign overruling secretly persists in a world in which countless things are done to God's dishonour and pain. He never made a child cry or a prisoner scream. He is Life not death, a Father not a fiend, and he calls us to turn to him, to trust him, to follow him. Every good gift comes from him,[17] he still sends his rain 'upon the righteous and the unrighteous',[18] but he does so to give us space for repentance[19] before a judgement which will come soon enough.[20]

Meanwhile, he continues to be God, creator, sustainer, provider and above all saviour; Father, Son and Spirit, to whom his children can look for provision and protection in redeemed lives which have their appointed destiny in him. Those lives are governed even now, not by blind fate but by a far-sighted providence which sees our future joys and steadfastly leads us to them. He is every day and every hour the God who can work in all things, great and small, in all events, good and bad, in all people, reconciled and hostile, 'for the good of those who love him, who have been called according to his purpose'.[21] This has been the glad experience of God's people from Joseph in the Old Testament[22] to Paul in the New.[23] It is the provision of God that covers the life-style of the sparrow and counts the hairs of our heads. It is the concern of Jehovah Jireh – our provider.

Notes

1 Ps. 145:13–16.
2 Matt. 6:25–34.
3 Matt. 6:34.
4 Shakespeare, *Julius Caesar*, I.ii. 134.
5 Isa. 45:1–7; 46:8–10.
6 Gen. 3:1–20.
7 Rom. 8:1–4, 18–21; Gal. 3:13.
8 Acrs 17:30–1.
9 Rev. 21:4.
10 e.g. Lam. 3:1–33.
11 Acts 2:23.
12 Cf. Acts 4:28.
13 e.g. Ps. 22:1–31; Isa. 53:6, 10; cf. Luke 24:27, 44–5.
14 Hab. 1:12–13; Eph. 1:11; 1 John 1:5.
15 Hab. 2:3.
16 Hab. 2:14.
17 Jas. 1:17.
18 Matt. 5:45.
19 Rom. 2:4–5.
20 2 Pet. 3:8–9.
21 Rom. 8:28.
22 Gen. 45:4–11.
23 Phil. 1:12–14.

AN INVITATION TO CONTENTMENT

There is an old story about an English lord who was passing the kitchens in his stately home one day and heard his cook, clearly distressed, say to her assistant, 'Oh, if only I had five pounds.' Because he appreciated her work, he walked into the room and gave the astonished woman her five pounds. Then he pretended to leave the area but hung around within earshot to catch her reaction. When she thought he had gone, he heard her say in exasperated tones to her companion, 'Drat it! If I'd known I'd have said fifty!'

Contentment is not something which comes easily to us. Nor is it something which we find easy to keep when we have it. We speak of 'finding contentment' as if it lay waiting to be discovered or hiding elusively while we hunt for it. We are sure that we will be content in the next job or the next house, or with the next car or the new furniture. But, like the carrot tied to the donkey, it will always be just out of reach for as long as we think of it in that way.

For contentment depends on an inner quality, not just on an outward condition. It rises within us from a recognition that what we have is more valuable than what we do not have, and that what we lack in ourselves can never be made up from what we may acquire in the world around us.

The apostle Paul makes just this point when he tells his Philippian readers:

> I have learned to be content whatever the circumstances. I know what it is to be in need, and I know what it is to have plenty. I have learned the secret of being content in any and every situation, whether well

fed or hungry, whether living in plenty or in want. I can do everything through him who gives me strength.[1]

The word Paul uses there which is translated 'content' was a word used in the ancient world by the philosophers to describe the 'self-sufficient' man; that is, the man who made himself independent of circumstances and had sufficient strength within himself to meet all circumstances calmly. Hence the New English Bible translation of verse 11, 'I have learned to find resources in myself whatever my circumstances.' Unlike the philosophers, however, Paul traces this self-sufficiency to the indwelling Spirit of Christ; as he puts it, 'I can do everything through him who gives me strength.'[2] Peter O'Brien comments: 'He was not so much self-sufficient as God-sufficient.'[3]

There are lessons here for us all. Every man and woman lives in two worlds – an external world and an internal world. The external world is the world of action; the internal world is the world of identity. Often, however, we confuse these two worlds and 'find' our identity solely in the external world of actions and circumstances. A man or woman gets wealth, power, prestige in the outer world and imagines that they *are* that image, that reputation, that life-style. They place their identity in their success, promotion, popularity, achievement, luxury. Then, when they are stripped of these (or fail to achieve them), they are disorientated, dismayed, they suffer an identity crisis, they fall into despair. Their resources were all outside themselves, and when these were taken away there was nothing left from which to draw comfort, support and reassurance.

But this is tragic, and the more so because it is unnecessary. The man, the woman, are in themselves so much more important and significant than all those other things. We are always bigger than our gains, bigger than our successes – or lack of success. One believer who had been rich and then, through no fault of his own, had lost everything, still retained his joy and peace as a Christian. When asked how he could remain so much the same after his misfortune as before it, he replied with beautiful wisdom: 'When I was rich I had God in everything. Now that I am poor I have everything in God.' That was Paul's triumph and it can be ours.

This does not mean, of course, that our outward lives and their achievements are unimportant. God gives us gifts and we should use them. God gives success in many things at many points in our lives and we can celebrate it. It is neither natural nor spiritual to be indifferent to success or failure, and Paul does not say otherwise. He learned not to be *indifferent* but to be *content*, and there is a world of difference between the two. He is a grateful, trusting Christian, not a passionless stone!

Nor does this mean that the losses and crosses of life are easy to bear. The grace of contentment is not an anaesthetic which numbs the pains of life, but an attitude which can cope with life's losses and its gains, its burdens and its comforts. This mind-set and spirit is learned only gradually and sometimes painfully.

Paul makes it clear that this was his own experience. Twice over he says, 'I have learned' this, 'I have learned the secret'. No doubt Paul, the man of action, had often chafed at delay; no doubt with the expectations of zeal he had found it as hard as any of us would do to deal equably with disgrace and honour. Character, like coral, is built up only little by little. It is by a thousand small victories that the war is won. How we meet each day's events, pressures and opportunities; how we respond to events we cannot control (for while events may lie beyond our control, our response to them does not); and how the experiences of life, good and bad, leave us, will determine whether we, as the years unfold, will have learned what Paul learned. If we do, we shall have learned a valuable lesson, we shall be rich, not poor, we shall have acquired what an old writer calls 'The rare jewel of Christian contentment'.

As to the supply of our daily needs: just as we have learned that God is aware of them, that he is concerned about them, that he has been supplying them on a pretty regular basis for millions of us, every day and through long years, so we can look to him and rest in him to continue to do what he has so graciously and lovingly and faithfully done. Our daily bread is not to be our daily worry, even if it is our daily prayer.

However, there is one more thing to be said in this regard: this prayer is for our need, not our greed. It is not a prayer for the finest wines or the richest cuisine but for the basics of life. These may be our legitimate concern – the rest is God's to give but not ours to expect. 'Having food to eat and clothes to wear let us therewith be content.'[4] Such an attitude comes most easily from those who know how little they deserve and how much they have been forgiven. For while this is 'the children's prayer', it is the prayer of sinners too. How impudent our 'shopping list prayers' are, as we ask for this and expect that and almost demand the other! To be sure, God is not begrudging in his forgiveness and our justification is complete in Christ. Yet as those who are still tottering in their holy walk, stammering and stumbling in their conversations with their Father, sinfully anxious one hour and sinfully confident the next, we need to learn the humility which seeks not what we want but what God wants for us, what he knows we can cope with, what he knows is best for his glory and for our good. I have long valued the wisdom in this prayer of an old churchman – and often smiled at the last line:

Lord, though such temporal enjoyments may seem good and desirable to me at present, yet thou art infinitely wise and knowest what the consequence of them will be. I ask for them if they may stand with thy will and if thou seest they will be as really good for me as I suppose them to be. If they be not so, I beg the favour of a denial.[5]

Have you learned to 'beg the favour of a denial'?

Notes

1 Phil. 4:11–13.
2 Phil. 4:13.
3 Peter O'Brien, *The Epistle to the Philippians*, Grand Rapids, Michigan, William B. Eerdmans, 1991, p. 521.
4 1 Tim. 6:8 (AV).
5 Ezekiel Hopkins, *Works*, 1701, p. 751.

AN INVITATION TO OUTRAGE

Every year 13 million children under the age of five die, many of hunger-related causes. Worldwide 190 million children under five are severely malnourished. More than one-fifth of the world's population (one billion human beings) is without adequate food, safe water, basic health-care & primary education. There is sufficient food in the world for everyone to receive about 2,500 calories each day, but many people are unable to buy food and distribution of supplies is grossly unequal.

God has given enough food on this planet to feed everyone; enough energy to serve everyone; enough people, power and progress to reach everyone. Given our world as it is, however, the problems of meeting world-wide need are immense. The greatest enemies remain apathy and despair, selfishness and greed, hatred and war. The roots of these lie in the heart of all mankind. The problem is not a God who does not care but a race which will not share.

Corruption and sin are not only in one place. The West has blushed at its butter-mountains and meat-mountains, its wine-lakes, its milk poured away and its wheat stocks burned, and at its economic explanations and moral discomfort. Yet many under-developed countries have leaders (the 'lootocracy') who siphon off economic aid to keep their 'gangs' and armies happy; marketeers who steal and sell food which was given freely; unbribed officials who leave food rotting on quaysides while populations starve inland. And many now downtrodden would love to have their hour of power!

Poverty devalues the human being, degrades human dignity and disfigures human spirituality, often driving people to sin and to crime. Poverty due to political maladministration, social bias and lack of opportunity offends God, degrades people and should outrage the Christian. Systems do need to be reformed, prejudice does need to be corrected, indifference does need to be challenged. And the Christian Church and individual Christians in the market-place and in high places of influence and trust should be outstanding and outspoken in their generation. In his book on Amos, Roy Clements writes:

> We have got to get out of the individualistic cast of mind which thinks we are responsible only for the things we have personally done against the Ten Commandments. It is much bigger than that. We are part of a world that has gone wrong and we share its guilt. A religion that is obsessed with personal holiness but which is content to let society go to the dogs is not based on true repentance; it is just self-indulgent pietism . . . There has to be that social dimension to our repentance.[1]

John Stott in his book *Issues facing Christians today* notes three types of 'poor' in Old Testament life: *the indigent poor* who are deprived of the basic necessities of life; *the oppressed poor* who are powerless victims of human injustice, and *the humble poor* who acknowledge their helplessness and look to God for salvation. Here economic, sociological and spiritual categories may overlap. The lessons of the Bible are that God sees, understands and reacts to these conditions. To quote Stott: 'God succours the indigent poor, champions the powerless poor and exalts the humble poor.'[2]

The challenge to us is that he seeks to do this through us, to become visible in us and to be effective by means of us. John Stott insists that in the light of Biblical revelation and in the sight of world-wide poverty Christians must modify their life-styles: 'We cannot maintain a "good life" (of extravagance) and a "good conscience" simultaneously. One or another has to be sacrificed. Either we keep our conscience and reduce our affluence or we keep our affluence and smother our conscience. We have to choose between God and mammon.'[3]

Stott does not call us to artificial or unrealistic extremes but he does call us to cultivate generosity, simplicity and contentment. Similarly, Paul does not command us to poverty, but he does command us to generosity when he writes to Timothy: 'Command those who are rich in this present world not to be arrogant nor to put their hope in wealth. . . . Command them to do good, to be rich in good deeds and to be generous and willing to share.'[4]

The prayer 'Give us today our daily bread' is significantly plural, and we can surely with good reason sometimes think of it as: 'Give them this day their daily bread'. In that case we can be part of the answer to the prayer we are praying. In a letter to *The Times* a few years ago, the Director of the Charities Aid Foundation wrote on charitable giving in Britain at large:

> Only a handful of people (mostly church-goers) give more than £20 per month – perhaps 5% of the population. Some 47% give £1 a month or less. The people in the prosperous South give not only a lesser percentage of their income to charity but less in total than people elsewhere. Companies give only about 0.2% of their pre-tax profits . . . private giving is therefore still light years behind the rhetoric which encourages it.[5]

An age-old response to this on the part of God's people has been the tithe: the devotion of one-tenth of one's income to religious or charitable purposes. It began as a point of honour with Abraham,[6] became a matter of Israelite law under Moses[7] and remains, I believe, as an evangelical challenge in this gospel age. In the New Testament we are encouraged to give not out of legal obligation but as a glad and grateful response,[8] and especially in recollection of the complete self-giving of Christ, who 'though he was rich, yet for your sakes

123

he became poor, so that you through his poverty might become rich.'[9] Such giving brings glory to God and the blessing of those helped upon those who have helped them.[10]

Yet beyond regular giving a needy world calls for extraordinary times of giving too. Our TV screens in recent years have shown us terrible scenes of hunger and distress, from Ethiopia to Rwanda. It is a time for extraordinary response from governments and individuals, as pot-bellied children and weak mothers and skeletal young men and the dying aged cry out of our screens to us: 'Give us today our daily bread'. No doubt we feel very helpless before the enormity of the problem, and God does not lay upon us the evil of the world. He does call us, however, to work with him to alleviate its misery for someone somewhere in some way. When someone told Mother Teresa that her work on the streets of Calcutta was a drop in the ocean, she famously replied that even the ocean was made up of drops.

I like the story of the freak wave that cast hundreds of fish on a stretch of shore-line. One man was seen desperately running from one to another, carrying them to the safety of the water. 'But there are hundreds!' cried a passer-by. 'What difference can you hope to make?' 'Well, it's made all the difference in the world to the ones I've rescued,' was the reply!

Notes

1 Roy Clements, *Where love and justice meet*, Leicester, IVP, 1988, p. 81.
2 John Stott, *Issues facing Christians today*, Basingstoke, Marshalls, 1984, p. 220.
3 Stott, p. 226.
4 1 Tim. 6:17–18.
5 Letter to *The Times*, Oct 14th 1988.
6 Gen. 14:20.

7 Mal. 3:6–18.
8 2 Cor. 8:1–5.
9 2 Cor. 8:9.
10 2 Cor. 9:12–15; cf. Matt. 5:16.

IV. FORGIVE US OUR DEBTS AS WE ALSO HAVE FORGIVEN OUR DEBTORS

31

OUR PROBLEM

Here we move from bread to forgiveness. Jesus takes us from what is essential for physical life to what is essential for eternal life. Here he reminds us of our greatest dignity and our greatest danger: namely, that we were made for eternal fellowship with God our creator but we have sinned and made ourselves liable to his wrath as judge. Yet he does not leave us under condemnation, but gives us a prayer which carries with it an implicit readiness in God to forgive and to restore us to our first destiny. Without this our lives would indeed be lived under the shadow of a great despair. What would bread be without forgiveness – or riches or power or prestige or long life be without peace with God? In the unforgettable words of Jesus as translated in the Authorised Version: 'What is a man profited, if he shall gain the whole world, and lose his own soul?'[1]

An essential characteristic of the Christian message is the quite unique stress it lays upon the matter of sin: its nature and its descents, its seriousness and its effects, and God's way of salvation in Christ Jesus. That message begins 'All have sinned and fall short of the glory of God' and ends with 'God made him who had no sin to be sin for us, so that in him we might become the righteousness of God.'[2] Dr J.I. Packer has written:

If you have not learned about sin, you cannot understand yourself or your fellow men, or the world in which you live or the Christian faith. And you will not be able to make head or tail of the Bible. For the Bible is an exposition of God's answer to the problem of human sin, and unless you have that problem clearly before you, you will keep missing the point of what it says.[3]

Apart from the biblical revelation and explanation, we shall review with growing puzzlement and exasperation our human history and our daily newspapers and our own hearts, as we try to understand why we just can't 'get it right'.

The Bible represents the sinful state of men and women by many different pictures or metaphors. For instance, we are said to be:

> *polluted* by our sin needing to be washed
> *in slavery* to sin needing to be freed
> *asleep* in our sins needing to be awakened
> *diseased* by sin needing to be healed
> *dead* in sin needing to be raised

In all these figures of speech the message is clear: we cannot help or save ourselves; we need nothing less than God to save us. Here in the Lord's Prayer we are said to be *debtors* on account of sin, utterly unable to pray what we owe, God's free forgiveness our only hope.

This is a debt which burdens everyone, God's goodness notwithstanding. We are debtors but not because God is a hard taskmaster or creditor. James reminds his readers that 'every good and perfect gift' is from 'the Father of the heavenly lights'.[4] However, our racial godlessness and past rebellion, our thoughtlessness and casual ingratitude, have long since turned *gifts* into *debts*, daily bread into daily contraband, blessings stolen and traded in lives which are alienated from the rule of God.

We still speak of a person's 'debt' to society when they are imprisoned for breaking the law of the land. Scripture tells us that God too has a law: not an arbitrary or even utilitarian code of required behaviour, but a law proceeding from his own essential being and nature as 'holy'. God's law proceeding from his righteousness, justice and truth requires perfect obedience. We, his unique creation, owe him all obedience in thought and word and deed: glad recognition of his goodness, willing conformity to his standards, instant response to his requirements: in a word, full and perfect obedience to all his laws. This is what we owe, what unfallen angels give as the very stuff of their existence, but what we are now disabled from doing by our own fault and folly, both individually and as a race.[5]

We have transgressed that law times without number and the burden of our debts has grown by the year. Sin unrepented and unforgiven does not diminish with time any more than old debts unpaid, which in fact grow with interest. Like unscrupulous businessmen we may hide our bankruptcy behind a facade of talent, style and achievements, but none of them can deal with or even diminish the huge bill of debts we have run up with God our maker and our judge.

Our sins affect others too. No one sins for themselves alone. Our dishonesties cheat others, our immoralities corrupt and compromise others, theft and violence leave scars on the mind as well as the body.

The effects of sin spread wider than we like to think. As factory and industrial smoke in England can kill trees in Norway by producing acid rain, so one generation's permissive and cynical fashions in morality and gross materialism can corrupt another, polluting its young growth with the acids of their own callous selfishness, sick humour and amoral propaganda.[6]

None of us knows the total effect of our sins or indeed of any particular sin for, as Paul Tournier has somewhere put it, 'The high drama of evil is that it cannot be localised.'

Roy Hessian tells the following story:

A saintly African Christian once told a congregation that as he was climbing the hill to the meeting he turned and saw a man carrying a very heavy load up the hill on his back. He was full of sympathy for him and spoke to him. He noticed that his hands were scarred and he realised that it was Jesus. He said to him, 'Lord, are you carrying the world's sin up the hill?' 'No,' said the Lord Jesus, 'not the world's sin, just yours!'[7]

131

Notes

1 Matt. 16:26.
2 Rom. 3:23; 2 Cor. 5:21.
3 J.I. Packer, *God's Words*, Leicester, IVP, 1981, p.71.
4 Jas. 1:17.
5 Rom. 3:9–20; 5:12; 8:6–8.
6 Prov. 9:13–18.
7 Roy Hessian, *The Calvary road*, London C.L.C., 1974, p. 36.

32

GOD'S SOLUTION

The gospel is about God's solution to humanity's greatest problem. That problem was entirely ours in respect of sin and guilt, but God made it his in respect of forgiveness and reconciliation. That God should love is not surprising, for God is love. That God should love sinners is astonishing, for God is holy and God's holiness includes his utter incompatibility with anything corrupt, anything unrighteous, in his creation. How then can God love sinners, how can he forgive sins, how can he be just and the one who 'justifies the ungodly'?[1]

John Stott, in *The cross of Christ*, quotes Carnegie Simpson, 'Forgiveness to man is the plainest of duties; to God it is the profoundest of problems', and carefully unpacks the second half of that statement:

> The obstacle to forgiveness is neither our sin alone nor our guilt alone but also the divine reaction in love and wrath towards guilty sinners. For although indeed 'God is love' yet we have to remember that his love is 'holy love', love which yearns over sinners while at the same time refusing to condone their sin. How, then, could God express his holy love? . . . Confronted by human evil, how could God be true to himself as holy love?[2]

The astonishing message of the New Testament is that God himself in holy love took personal responsibility for all our sins, for the payment of all our debts, for the satisfaction of his own justice. In the words of John Stott again, 'He bore the judgement we deserve in order to bring us the forgiveness we do not deserve.'[3]

The cross of Calvary is the focal point of that work. There he died, 'the righteous for the unrighteous, to bring you to God'.[4] There he became 'the atoning sacrifice for our sins, and not only for ours but also for the sins of the whole world'.[5] There God demonstrates his own love for us in this: 'While we were still sinners, Christ died for us',[6] 'God made him who had no sin to be sin for us, so that in him we might become the righteousness of God.'[7]

The reconciliation that flows from that act and its achievement is the central proclamation of the New Testament. As Paul says, 'God was reconciling the world to himself in Christ, not counting men's sins against them. And he has committed to us the message of reconciliation.'[8]

Martin Luther used to tell of a dream he once had in which Satan, the Accuser, presented Luther with a long scroll on which his sins were written. There they were, accurately and indelibly recorded: thoughts, words, deeds – of omission and commission – with dates, times and circumstances. Nothing was left out and they almost completely filled up the scroll from top to bottom. But at the bottom a space remained. And Luther, after Satan had recited them all, calmly and solemnly replied: 'Now write in the space at the bottom: "The blood of Jesus Christ, God's Son, cleanses us from all sin!"'[9]

At this point we must perhaps consider two questions.

People sometimes ask, 'Why do we need to pray for forgiveness each day if we are forgiven our sins from the start of our new life in Christ? Isn't our first forgiveness enough?'

Now we must answer that carefully. You see, if that first forgiveness is not enough for our eternal salvation, and if our justification is incomplete at our first entry into Christ as his people, then we could have no peace or joy as Christians, only fear and trepidation and anxiety. We would be afraid every day of losing our salvation; anxious that we had failed to maintain some standard, never gaining full assurance of salvation and safety in Christ. But that is not the New Testament picture of the Christian life, which is to be a life of assurance, joyful certainty that whatever happens to us we are safe in God, saved in Christ his Son.

So, what do we as believers have here in the daily prayer 'Forgive us our sins'? Not a reference to our decisive justification, our definitive state of salvation; but a reference *within that* to our state of closeness to God, cleanness before God, communion with God.[10] The forgiveness sought is not the removal of damnation but the restoration of fellowship with God. For sin is of such a nature and God is of such a nature that, though he will not now damn us because of our sins, he will and does chastise us for our sins; and for us the worst chastisement of all is to feel his absence, to sense his grief and anger.[11].

For the true Christian it is not enough to be saved from hell. We want to walk with God; to be close to God. But our sins disturb that intimacy, that communion, and may disturb our peace. We do not cease to be children of God – we can still pray 'Our Father'; but we are like children locked out, kept at a distance, the show of affection withdrawn, and so we pray 'forgive us our sins' as a much-loved child comes in sorrow to be drawn close by a loving parent. Mere forgiveness is not enough – we want forgiveness with kisses, forgiveness and our Father's face.

Secondly, people are often puzzled by the additional words '. . . as we also have forgiven our debtors'. Is this an attempt at a trade-off, our forgiveness of others traded for God's forgiveness of us? Of course not. It can't be. Our forgiveness is always incomplete: we are sinners in everything. And certainly we cannot *earn* forgiveness at any level. Salvation is all of grace. It is free. It is God's gift.

But Jesus does not say, 'Forgive us *on the grounds* of the fact that we forgive our debts' but 'forgive us *as we also* have forgiven'. Here is one of the signs that we belong to God, that he is our Father, that his Son is our Saviour and Lord, that his Spirit lives in us. These words 'as we also have forgiven' are the cry of the children telling the Father that they are on his side, that they belong to him, that they want to be more like him in purity and righteousness. It is one of the signs that we are among those who have already been forgiven in terms of justification but who also need daily forgiveness in terms of peace and assurance, the sense of the Father's 'Well done' and the well-being of those who keep short accounts with God and desire to 'go and sin no more'.

Those who never forgive, on the other hand, have never understood God or themselves. Leon Morris in his *Matthew* quotes a fellow writer: 'If anyone says "I'll never forgive you!" that person "is not penitentially aware of his sins, but only vengefully aware of another man's sins".'[12] Remember Jesus's parable about the steward who would not forgive his underling even though his master had forgiven him a far greater debt.[13]

The spur that makes you love much is the sense that *you* have been loved much. And your love will tell its own tale of sins forgiven.[14] But if your heart is not open to pour out love it is simply not open for God to pour in love. Let God your Father, in the same act of pouring his love *into* your heart, pour his love *through* your heart into other hearts. And let those hearts include those who might have expected no love from you whom they injured, in order that they may hope for love and forgiveness from God whom they have long opposed.

But if we see sin here in the prayer not as the guilt that damns but as the sin that spoils communion with God, then it further holds true that full and free fellowship with God will not be enjoyed by the Christian believer until he or she seriously and deliberately and openly forgives those who have sinned against them. That is not an easy work – but it does bring great freedom, great reward, great demonstrations of love from a heavenly Father who is growing his children into the likeness of Christ Jesus, who is himself the likeness of God: God who gives – and forgives every day of our lives.

Notes

1 Rom. 4:5 (AV).

2 John Stott, *The cross of Christ*, Leicester, IVP, 1986, pp. 88–9.
3 Stott, p. 89.
4 1 Pet. 3:18.
5 1 John 2:2.
6 Rom. 5:8.
7 2 Cor. 5:21.
8 2 Cor. 5:19.
9 1 John 1:7–10; 2:1–2.
10 John 13:10; 14:23; 17:21, 23.
11 Ps. 51: 7–12.
12 Leon Morris, *Matthew*, Leicester, IVP, 1992, p. 147, quoting G. A. Buttrick.
13 Matt. 18:21–35.
14 Luke 7:41–7.

ON OUR KNEES AND IN HIS ARMS

There is a touching story, told originally by Dr. Barnardo himself, of how a dirty, ragged urchin approached him nervously in the street one day asking that he might be taken into one of Barnardo's homes. 'I know nothing about you, my lad,' said the Doctor, 'What have you in the way of recommendation?' 'Please sir, I thought these would be enough,' murmured the little chap, pointing to his rags. Dr. Barnardo gathered him up in his arms and took him in.

Jesus offers himself to sinners, others need not apply: 'I have not come to call the righteous but sinners to repentance.'[1] He calls us as we are, that he might one day make us as we should be. He calls us to come in our rags, with our failures, whispering to him the things we can tell to no one else. And he takes us in, not as orphans but as dearly-loved children, not as servants but as sons and daughters, not as barely-saved but as fully-reconciled. And while repentance has to be renewed every day (for we are daily sinners) so is his forgiveness, cleansing and renewing available every day.[2]

Let us however look more closely now at these themes of repentance, faith and forgiveness.

The call of God in the gospel is to *repentance* for sin[3] and *faith* in Jesus Christ as Saviour and Lord.[4] Repentance is quite simply turning to God in sorrow and self-giving. It is not mere regret; feeling sorry that you have committed a sin is not repenting of sin. To reduce repentance to a mood is to lose sight of its life-changing character. Repentance is a change of mind issuing from a change of heart and leading to a change of life. It is a turning towards the light with all that that implies for the creeping things of darkness: the pride, jealousy and lust that lurk and lodge in dark corners of all our hearts. It is an exposure to God which has incalculable and abiding effects. It is a change of thought and purpose in which a radically new assessment of life is made, with a full and sincere purpose to live to God and walk in his ways. It does not end at conversion but continues and is renewed throughout life.

We can see from this that true repentance is no casual or easy thing. Such is our chronic doubt and double-mindedness that even our repentance needs to be repented of. Yet where God is at work a spirit of humility and sorrow for sin rises within us. Indeed repentance is God's gift before it is his demand, and we should go to God for it even when we feel we cannot go to God *with* it. God starts where we are and helps us with the first and most tentative steps. This should be a great encouragement to the weakest believer.

Repentance involves confession, and confession is the acknowledging of our sin, our fault, our debt before God. This is not easy since we are very prone to excuse ourselves and to blame others. But we shall not find the relief we most need and which God offers unless we take responsibility for our wrong-doings. We hear a lot these days about 'self-discovery', 'self-understanding' and 'self-affirmation'. But we never truly discover ourselves by disguising ourselves. Jesus faces us with our sin, our guilt, our need of him. Yet in doing so he does not rubbish us; he gives us value! He is saying in effect 'Because you matter so much to me I am going to deal with you in grace and truth. I am going to accuse you and acquit you; to uncover your filthiness and wash you clean; to turn you from your rebel ways and reconcile you to myself for ever.'

This work of personal salvation can never be earned. It can only be received as a gift. The earning has been done by Christ Jesus. We have only to receive him and what he has done for us in repentance and faith. He is our righteousness,[5] 'a righteousness from God' which is gained, not by good works in any degree, but 'by faith from first to last'.[6] This alone is a righteousness that will survive the uncompromising judgements of God in the Day of Judgement:

> Bold shall I stand in that great Day
> For who aught to my charge will lay?
> Fully absolved through thee I am
> From sin and darkness guilt and shame.[7]

The joyful truth of justification by faith in Christ Jesus is that we do not have to wait in apprehension or uncertainty for that 'great Day'. For those who have surrendered themselves to Jesus Christ as Lord and Saviour, the verdict of the Day of Judgement has already gone out: '"Not Guilty" – for Jesus's sake. Accepted in the Beloved': 'Therefore, since we have been justified through faith, we have peace with God through our Lord Jesus Christ, through whom we have gained access by faith into this grace in which we now stand. And we rejoice in the hope of the glory of God.[8]

This 'faith', so crucial to the personal application of redemption, is not a merely human characteristic. Like repentance (which is its first expression) it is a gift from God.[9] Nor is it a synonym for credibility or superstition. As John Stott puts it, 'Faith is a reasonable trust.'[10] Nothing is more reasonable than that we should trust Jesus's claims and act upon his words. And faith is basically just such a trust: trusting oneself to him as Saviour and Lord in complete reliance on what he has done for our salvation, coming to him who will not drive us away[11] and surrendering to him in love and self-giving:

> Love so amazing, so divine,
> Demands my soul, my life, my all![12]

But this trust involves the recognition of our own need and utter insufficiency – and the inadequacy of any other help. As John Calvin famously put it: 'Faith is nothing more than the empty hand of the beggar receiving the bounty

of a giving God.' In this there must be the recognition of
our sins and the renunciation of self-righteousness. It is an
empty hand we must stretch out to God:

> Nothing in my hand I bring,
> Simply to Thy cross I cling:
> Naked, come to Thee for dress;
> Helpless, look to Thee for grace;
> Foul, I to the fountain fly:
> Wash me, Saviour, or I die![13]

This is the faith that turns in repentance to the God who
calls and to the Christ who saves. It is the Spirit's work of
new birth.[14]

The result of all this – the cancellation of debts, the
lifting of burdens, the forgiveness of sins – will affect more
lives than our own. If we know how much we are forgiven,
then we shall be the more ready to forgive others. If we
know we are loved – by God and to the utmost – then we
shall have a power to love that goes beyond any natural
inclination or moralising. If the joy of our salvation fills
us, it will overflow to others also.[15]

I like to quote a passage from John Masefield's poem
'The everlasting mercy'. It tells of the conversion of Saul
Kane, a man who had existed through a wild career of
coarseness, drinking and imprisonment: a squalid and
desperate life. There are some beautiful and powerful
lines capturing the encounter with God and Kane's
entry into a new world because Christ had made him
a new man:

> I did not think, I did not strive,
> The deep peace burnt my 'me' alive;
> The bolted door had broken in,
> I knew that I had done with sin.
> I knew that Christ had given me birth
> To brother all the souls on earth,
> And every bird and every beast
> Should share the crumbs broke at the feast.

O glory of the lighted mind
How dead I'd been, how dumb, how blind.
The station brook, to my new eyes,
Was bubbling out of Paradise;
The waters rushing from the rain
Were singing Christ has risen again.
I thought all earthly creatures knelt
From rapture of the joy I felt.[16]

Notes

1 Matt. 9:13.
2 1 John 1:8–9.
3 Acts 17:30.
4 Acts 2:38; 4:12.
5 1 Cor. 1:30.
6 Rom. 1:17.
7 'Jesus, thy robe of righteousness', Nicolaus Ludwig von Zinzendorf (1700–60), trans. John Wesley.
8 Rom. 5:1–2.
9 Acts 5:31; Eph. 2:8.
10 John Stott, quoted in Russell Chandler, *Understanding the new age*, Irving, Texas, Word Books, 1988, p. 312.
11 John 6:37.
12 'When I survey the wondrous cross', Isaac Watts (1674–1748).
13 'Rock of Ages, cleft for me', A.M. Toplady (1740–1778).
14 John 3:3, 5, 16; 1 John 5:1.
15 Mark 5:19–20; Luke 7:36–50; John 9:25.
16 John Masefield (1878–1967), 'The everlasting mercy', *The Collected Poems*, London, William Heinemann, 1924, p. 125.

GOD'S EXAMPLE

The forgiveness of God is so complete that writers of Scripture ransack their language for symbols strong enough and metaphors forceful enough to describe it. Micah cries:

> Who is a God like you, who pardons sin and forgives the transgression of the remnant of his inheritance? You do not stay angry for ever but delight to show mercy. You will again have compassion on us; you will tread our sins underfoot and hurl all our iniquities into the depths of the sea.[1]

One of the most joyful Psalms has this as the centre of its joys:

> He does not treat us as our sins deserve
>   or repay us according to our iniquities.
> For as high as the heavens are above the earth,
>   so great is his love for those who fear him;
> as far as the east is from the west,
>   so far has he removed our transgressions from us.[2]

Perhaps the most striking expression depicting the complete forgiveness of God is the image of God forgetting. Think of that! The power of the divine memory, like the power of the divine mind and will, is infinite. As a shepherd counts his sheep, so Yahweh counts the number of the stars 'and calls them each by name'.[3] Every atom and cell is held in being by him, every word is weighed and every thought laid bare; his omniscience is total. Yet he says through Jeremiah that a new day is approaching and a new covenant is going to come into operation: 'I will forgive their wickedness and will remember their sins no more.'[4]

'No power on earth' writes John White, 'can touch pardon. Atomic power can vaporise a city. It can raise a mushroom cloud miles into the sky. But it can neither soften a hardened heart, straighten the shoulders of a discouraged person nor break the power of sin.'[5]

We are among those whose hearts have been softened, whose shoulders have often been straightened, who have been given fresh courage and purpose in our lives because we have found forgiveness in God and received pardon full and free, ungrudging and unlimited. God whose Son Jesus taught us to forgive 'seventy times seven' is as good as his word – except that he has never counted! Someone once said, 'When we go to our Father grieving and anxious, confessing "Father, I've done it again," he replies, "What do you mean 'again'"?' It makes the point that he forgives *and forgets*. He does not bind us to our past.

That is what guilt does: it binds us to our sin, to an unforgiven past. We have a powerful illustration of that in the story of Joseph and his brothers in the Old Testament book of Genesis. At the climax of the story Joseph, now chief minister in Egypt, keeps his identity a secret from the brothers who wronged him. Pretending to believe they are spies, Joseph continues to keep one of them prisoner while the others go back to Canaan for the younger brother, Benjamin. We read: 'They said to one another, "Surely we are being punished because of our brother. We saw how distressed he was when he pleaded with us for his life, but we would not listen; that's why this distress has come upon us."'[6] You see the point? They are still loaded with the guilt of their sin committed years before; consequently, when calamity comes they immediately see it as retribution for their wrong-doing.[7] They are chained to their past, and no power can dissolve those chains. No power, that is, except the power of forgiveness. Joseph's tears dissolve their chains;[8] his love, his forgiveness and his faith in God[9] finally and definitively free them from their past and free them for a new future.

Here is a lesson for us all from Joseph's brethren. The past is not easily left behind. It has ongoing effects. It has built and shaped the present. We are just not strong enough to deal with the past and reshape the present. Like a once-supple sapling which has become a gnarled, unbending tree, we find our spirits stubborn, our passions too strong for us or our apathy too paralysing. We need a power that can forgive us completely and change us fundamentally.

It is confession and the prayer for forgiveness which open up the heart to the surge of love which comes from the Father-heart of God and beats against the doors and windows of a life, seeking entry. And when it gains it, the rush of cleansing that comes in clears us of the rubbish of years. But there can be no forgiveness where there is no repentance, no cleansing where the heart is sullen and sealed. Then our sins only accumulate, we stagger under a growing load of unconfessed wrong-doing; we hide it and absorb its pollution instead of washing it away. We justify ourselves and take shelter in the lie, and this lie becomes part of us and we of it and there is no shelter. Where then is the heart set free? Where is repentance to be found and the grace to pray in faith 'Father . . . forgive'? Not from ourselves but from God, and not from God in the skies but God on the cross; not from God reigning in glory but from God suffering at our hands and forgiving: 'When they came to the place called the Skull, there they crucified him, along with the criminals – one on his right, the other on his left. Jesus said, "Father, forgive them, for they do not know what they are doing."'[10]

We do not have to look very far to see who needs forgiveness most, and we do not have to look very far to see where forgiveness may be found. Here, at the cross, hearing such words of love to us even as our sins nail him there; here, if anywhere, we can confess our sins and seek forgiveness. Here, pride is sapped of its strength and cynicism forgets its lines. Here, God says the words for us and takes the blame for us: 'the punishment that brought us peace was upon him.'[11] It was because he 'bore the sin

145

of many, and made intercession for the transgressors'[12] that we can pray 'forgive us our debts for Jesus' sake'.

> The price is paid,
> Come let us enter in
> To all that Jesus died to make our own.
> For every sin
> More than enough He gave,
> And bought our freedom from each guilty stain.
> The price is paid, Alleluia,
> Amazing grace, so strong and sure
> And so with all my heart,
> My life in every part,
> I live to thank You for the price You paid.[13]

Notes

1 Mic. 7:18–19.
2 Ps. 103:10–12.
3 Ps. 147:4.
4 Jer. 31:34; cf. Heb. 10:16–17.
5 John White, *The Race*, Leicester, IVP, 1984, p. 157.
6 Gen. 42:21.
7 Gen. 42:22, 28; 44:16.
8 Gen. 45:2.
9 Gen. 45:4–8.
10 Luke 23:33–4.
11 Isa. 53:5.
12 Isa. 53:12.
13 'The price is paid', Graham Kendrick, Thank You Music, 1983.

GOD'S DEMAND

When God forgives us our sins against him the first thing he asks us to do is to forgive others their sins against us. This is a main part of love and Jesus said 'Love each other as I have loved you.'[1] Love is the master-work that God does at the centre of the believer's life. Here, settled in one disposition of the heart, in one overriding attitude, in one ruling power, is the imitation of Christ and the likeness of God. In this the image is restored more than in anything else. So vital is this that it forms an eleventh commandment[2] which sums up and embraces all the others. To love God and your neighbour as yourself is the foundation of new life which lives not only by the new commandment but in the power of him who gave it. For you cannot be legalistic here, even though love is the fulfilling of the law. And you cannot love nominally, any more than you can breathe only on special occasions: 'Dear friends, let us love one another, for love comes from God. Everyone who loves has been born of God and knows God. Whoever does not love does not know God, because God is love . . . Whoever loves God must also love his brother.'[3]

However, this does not mean that love is effortless for us. We are not yet in heaven and there are contradictory forces within us as well as around us.[4] We have the Spirit within us, planting and nurturing his fruit of love, joy, peace, patience etc.[5] But we still need the command to 'keep in step with the Spirit'.[6]

The apostle Paul works this out directly in terms of forgiveness and peace in the churches when he writes to the Colossian Christians: 'Therefore, as God's chosen people, holy and dearly loved, clothe yourselves with compassion, kindness, humility, gentleness and patience. Bear with

each other and forgive whatever grievances you may have against one another. Forgive as the Lord forgave you.'[7]
We do not find this an easy thing to do. Marion Ashton tells the story of one woman who went away deeply convicted after the preacher had spoken on this subject. The next day, when people were being asked to say ways in which they had been blessed, she said, 'Last night, when I got home I asked the Lord to help me to throw away my despisory.' She went on to say that she had realised that she kept something like a card index system at the back of her mind of all the things that people had done against her and for which she despised them.[8]

No doubt 'forgive and forget' may be easy enough when the injury is small and the attitude carefree. But when the injury is great or the sense of sin profound, there, in the moment of recoil, to embrace, to turn cursing into blessing and to seek the sinner behind and beyond the sin, there the victory is profound and the cost of it great. As Simon Tugwell puts it, 'Forgiveness is not something for nice people with weak stomachs!'[9]

I agree with those who say this is often a slow process and one that has to be repeated. Floyd McClung writes wisely:

Forgiveness is often a process and not a once only act. We keep on forgiving until the pain goes away. The deeper the wound the greater the forgiveness needed. Just as a doctor has to keep a physical wound in our bodies clean from infection so that this wound can heal properly so we must keep our emotional wounds clean of bitterness so they can heal. Forgiveness keeps the wounds clean. Whenever you think of a particular person and feel hurt, forgive them. Just tell the Lord that you forgive that person and that you choose to love them with God's love. Receive his love for them by faith, keep doing that every time you think of the person, until you feel God's love released in your heart for them.[10]

Rita Nightingale, falsely imprisoned in Thailand on a charge of smuggling heroin, writes of her attempts to forgive:

> It was a slow and painful progression. Each person had to be prayed over, agonised over and forgiven. When I thought I had really forgiven somebody I would find myself resenting them two or three days later and have to forgive them all over again. It was only as I looked back, as the days became weeks and the weeks months, that I saw my attitudes were changing. I was learning how to forgive.[11]

Here is the victory of faith, the triumph of love, the signature of God on our lives.

There is one person who never forgives because he never loves. That person is Satan. The word 'Satan' means 'adversary' and he is called 'the accuser of the brethren'.[12] Where he meets malice he re-enforces it; where he meets goodness he holds it in contempt; where he meets failure and sin in Christian lives he raises around them a storm of reproach and digs at their feet a pit of despair. He first tempts people into sin and then accuses them of sin. This is especially true of his dealings with God's people.[13] It includes, of course, people in the church who have sinned against us, people whom we are tempted (in turn) to hate or despise or resent. This brings us to a point of decision. When others have taken advantage of us, or let us down or spoken ill of us, we have a choice which to us should be no choice at all. I once heard Elizabeth Elliott say on forgiveness: 'You can either stand with Satan against that person or you can stand with Christ for them.'

We are never more like God than when we forgive. God himself delights in mercy and loves to forgive. When he revealed himself in his glory to Moses it was this self-description which was at the centre of his glory: 'And he passed in front of Moses, proclaiming, "The Lord, the Lord, the compassionate and gracious God, slow to anger, abounding in love and faithfulness, maintaining love to thousands, and forgiving wickedness, rebellion and sin.'"[14]

While he also warns the impenitent that 'he does not leave the guilty unpunished',[15] yet judgement is his 'strange work' his 'alien task'.[16] He delights in mercy[17] but grieves in judgement.[18]

It is our duty to forgive because it is God's command and because we ourselves have been forgiven, but it is also our privilege because it is God-like to forgive.[19] Alas, we would often prefer to be like God in judgement than to be like him in mercy, more aware of others' sins than our own, and always ready to qualify God's commands with exceptions or to say 'That's enough' when we've only just begun to obey.

The forgiving heart delights God. Many have felt the love and joy and peace of God flood their heart as they forgave, especially when that forgiveness was a hard and painful work, as it sometimes is. Nothing pleases the heart of God like mercy, forgiveness and love. Here he meets the beauty of his own image in us; here he meets the likeness of the Son he loves who prayed for his enemies; and here those around us meet with the sign of the future in the present, the promise of a new earth where love will face no contradiction. Even where your forgiveness has met with a poor response from your fellow human beings, get on your knees in a quiet place and let your Father embrace you and encourage you. Christ often whispers his 'Well done, good and faithful servant' *before* the final day!

It is also our disposition to forgive. It may be a struggle at times, but it is not only a struggle. The Christian heart is already the place 'wherein the Holy Spirit makes his dwelling'. There is a readiness to love and to forgive and to be reconciled to others. Anger and bitterness are not foods we can thrive on and we can never enjoy the after-taste of revenge. We have learned a better way of living, for God has changed our hearts and now we are different in action and reaction. We are fools to ourselves when we act as the world expects, for we are acting out of character and distancing ourselves from the God in whom we delight.

It is when we turn the sinful standards of the world on their heads and respond to our Father's very different rules that we astonish the world and perhaps seed hope in hearts long-hardened and cynical.

We have encouragements to forgive in every direction. The forgiving heart is the one that has found and entered upon a great freedom. The forgiving heart has no excuse not to forgive, there can be no refuge for bitterness in its wide landscape.[20] *When we look back* at our own sins and failure, our past ingratitude and present weakness, we should not be inclined to keep alive our own little resentments; but when we see how much we have been forgiven and how much we are loved, we may well entertain and cultivate a generous spirit towards others. *When we look up* to a Christ praying for us[21] and meet his prayers with our own to be more like him, we may well exchange resentments for prayers and pray for those who use us badly, just as he said when he was here on earth.[22] *When we look forward* to our eternal future of joy and glory and dare to contemplate the everlasting fate of those who ill-use God more than they ill-use us, we can soon feel pity more than resentment and be ready to lighten their load a little, of our recriminations at least. Perhaps the greatest encouragement is the possibility that our love in return for hatred will become the channel of a greater love and an irresistible grace, which will capture and rescue them from an eternal exclusion[23] and bring them to a Father's home.[24]

Notes

1 John 15:12.
2 John 13:34–5.
3 1 John 4:7–8, 21.
4 Gal. 5:17.
5 Gal. 5:22.
6 Gal. 5:25.
7 Col. 3:12–13.

8 Marion Ashton, *Growing into wholeness*, Eastbourne, Kingsway, 1985, p. 42.

9 Simon Tugwell, *Prayer*, Dublin, Veritas Pubs, 1974, p. 82.

10 Floyd McClung, *The Father heart of God*, Eastbourne, Kingsway, 1985, p. 93.

11 Rita Nightingale, *Freed for life*, Basingstoke, Marshall Pickering, 1982, p. 176.

12 Rev. 12:10 (AV).

13 Job 1:9–11; Zech. 3:1–5; Luke 22:31–4.

14 Exod. 34:6–7.

15 Exod. 34:7.

16 Isa. 28:21.

17 Mic. 7:18.

18 Luke 19:41–4.

19 Ps. 86:1–5.

20 Matt. 18:21–35.

21 Heb. 7:25.

22 Matt. 5:43–8.

23 Matt. 25:41–6.

24 Luke 15:18–24.

V. AND LEAD US NOT INTO TEMPTATION, BUT DELIVER US FROM THE EVIL ONE

36

SOVEREIGNTY AND SUCCOUR

'And lead us not into temptation but deliver us from the evil one.' In the original languages in which the Bible is written, the same word is used for both *testing* and *tempting*. God is often said to test his people to try to demonstrate the genuineness of their loyalty to him. This is testing with a good motive. On the other hand, Satan too is said to test the people of God – but with a view to undermining their faith and destroying their witness, and so bringing disgrace to the cause of God or the name of Christ. This is usually what we call temptation. Sometimes in the same event or life-experience both God and Satan are at work in different ways for different purposes: God testing, encouraging, strengthening for victory over temptation; Satan pressurising, seducing, weakening if he can and aiming at our defeat and downfall.

This part of the Lord's Prayer, therefore, is a plea by the Christian that he or she might not be led into such overwhelming temptation that they fall before the power of the evil one; a prayer that when temptation threatens, they may be delivered from it and from the devil who uses it.

In other words, it is a prayer for protection and strength, in which the believer knows their own weakness and vulnerability and confesses their daily, hourly need of God's grace and care.

Has God got anything to do with temptation in our lives? The surprising but also comforting answer of Scripture is 'Yes'! Of course it's true that God tempts no one in the way that Satan does, and we cannot blame God when we fail in testing times or situations. As James says, we have to accept responsibility for what we do: 'When tempted, no one should say, "God is tempting me." For God cannot be tempted by evil, nor does he tempt anyone; but each one is tempted when, by his [or her] own evil desire, he is dragged away and enticed.'[1]

Yet the Scriptures also make it quite clear that God has an overall sovereignty in life which never leaves him on the sidelines. He is at the heart of every event and experience of our lives, even of suffering, when he suffers with us, and of temptation, when he stays close to us. And in his time he delivers us from evil.

There is a sense in which God does indeed lead his people into testing situations where they will be tempted. We have a very clear instance of that in the life of Christ. After the account of Jesus' baptism we read: 'Then Jesus was led by the Spirit into the desert to be tempted by the devil.'[2]

Isn't it important for us to know this? Isn't it important in the *tests* of life and at the points of great *pressure* and *temptation* to know that God is in control, that he is still leading us, that he will not let us be tempted above our strength and that he will lead us out into victory and freedom?

But why, you may ask, does God allow it all in the first place? Are we just bit-players in the cast of some cosmic pantomime without real meaning or value except to some over-worked angels who need to watch a good soap opera?

No, life is for real, and the Bible deals with the real world. It gives us thoughtful and weighty reasons why God allows his people to go through hard times of assault, of suffering and setback and of temptation. They are not simple answers to complex issues, but they are real ingredients, crucial elements in the spiritual warfare. They comfort us and they strengthen us.

Sometimes God allows us to be tested to show his own commitment and keeping power in our lives. And so the Psalmist often celebrates God as his refuge and fortress, his shield and protector.[3]

Sometimes he allows us to be tested to show the truth and quality of his grace in us and our faith in him[4] and to enable us to reassure others.[5] Who would have heard of Job or been helped by his story if Job had not suffered at Satan's hands?[6]

Sometimes God uses such times and even our falls to humble us and warn others, even as he humbled the overconfident Peter, who caved in to fear and denied his Lord.[7]

Sometimes God does it to make us more understanding towards others – and more approachable, too. I think it was the English preacher F.B. Meyer who once said that when we see a brother or a sister in sin, we should remember that there are three things we do not know: first, we do not know how hard he or she tried not to sin; second, we do not know the power of the forces that assailed him or her; and third, we do not know what we would have done in the same circumstances. Paul says: 'Brothers, if someone is caught in a sin, you who are spiritual should restore him gently. But watch yourself, or you also may be tempted. Carry each other's burdens . . .'[8]

It may seem odd to say it, but sometimes God can even use temptation to save us from sin. Strong temptations sometimes frighten us, showing us what we could be or do without God's power and protection. And so we become more wary of situations which we should avoid in future. Often we would sin more if we were tempted less!

One thing we can be sure of: God may bring us into testing times and hard conflict, but he will always be with us there. He may lead us into temptation, but he will never leave us in temptation and he will in his own time deliver us out of our trial:

Fear not, for I have redeemed you; I have summoned you by name; you are mine. When you pass through the waters, I will be with you; and when you pass through the rivers, they will not sweep over you. When you walk through the fire, you will not be burned; the flames will not set you ablaze.[9]

Notes

1 Jas. 1:13–14.
2 Matt. 4:1.
3 e.g. Ps. 3–7.
4 Job 1:1, 8, 21.
5 2 Cor. 1:4.
6 Job 1:12; 2:6; 23:10; cf. 1 Pet. 1:7.
7 Luke 22:31–4; cf. 1 Pet. 5:5–6.
8 Gal. 6:1.
9 Isa. 43:1–2.

TEMPTATION AS TESTING

Coloured water can look like wine until you drink it. A car can look sound enough until you drive it. People can seem pleasant and unselfish or stable and helpful until you get to know them or need them. So also, people can have the name of Christian without any personal experience of Christ's love and power, without a new heart and a new inner principle of Godliness.[1]

Even in the Old Testament period God taught the difference between being *nominally* in his covenant and belonging *personally* to him. So again and again we read that God tests his own people, Israel, to 'see' (really to show) whether or not they will be true to their place in the covenant. He tested Abraham to show the supreme quality of his faith.[2] He tested Israel in the wilderness to show his own faithfulness and to bring to light both their loyalty and their unfaithfulness.[3] He tested the nation in Canaan by keeping them in proximity to alternative religions and life-styles with the command to be separate as his holy people.[4]

Notice how God is said to test his own people, not the nations around them. They do not belong to him, but Israel does.[5] We need to understand that such testing in our own lives is not the mark of his wrath but the mark of his love; it is not the evidence of his abandonment but the sign of our sonship and daughterhood and his commitment to us. To the nominal believer it is a test which exposes their hypocrisy, but to the true believer it is a discipline which refines, matures and develops them. So the Psalmist can say after a testing time: 'Before I was afflicted I went astray, but now I obey your word . . .' and 'It was good for me to be afflicted so that I might learn your decrees.' The experience has made him value God more than ever:

'The law from your mouth is more precious to me than thousands of pieces of silver and gold.'[6]

Times of *persecution for our faith* are outstanding times of testing when stern realities are faced, priorities set at all costs and personal weaknesses, such as fear, doubt and selfishness, faced and dealt with as never before. In a prayer letter during the Communist ascendancy a few years back, a Russian believer wrote:

> My first fifteen-day sentence taught me a great deal about myself. In such a situation you see your good and bad points very clearly. You find out where your weaknesses are. Persecution can be compared to a photographic developer. When the film is immersed in the developer an image appears. When a Christian encounters persecution his character becomes evident. Our church quickly learned who was ready for persecution and who wasn't.

A wise old man once said to a young Chinese Christian: 'A man's faith is like a teabag. It's only in hot water that it shows its true colour!' This is a consistent New Testament perspective on times of trial and loss for Christ's cause.[7]

Often the tests consist in *prolonged trials* which 'stretch' us. We recognise that we are not immune from the ills and pressures of life; we are prepared to take our share of suffering like good soldiers of Christ,[8] but then we discover that our share is rather larger than we expected, the test is greater, the trial longer, the expectation on God's part greater, and we begin to protest. 'That's enough now, Lord,' we say, 'I've learned the lesson', 'I've got the message', 'I'm sure I'm better equipped to help others and testify to your all-sufficiency, please stop now!' But God doesn't stop – the pressures and demands increase, and we remind God that he has promised not to try us above our strength. But he says we've more strength than we know. After a while, we protest that we're at our last gasp – but he simply replies, 'Oh no, you've got a few more gasps in you yet.' And we always have! And somehow we not only survive but come out conquerors, though we might scarcely know it.

Oswald Chambers somewhere has put it memorably:

> A saint's life is in the hands of God like a bow and arrow in the hands of our maker. God is aiming at something the saint cannot see and he stretches and strains and every now and again the saint says 'I cannot stand any more'. God does not heed but goes on stretching till his purpose is in sight. Then he lets fly. Trust yourself in God's hands.[9]

Often the test consists in *great loss*: the onset of a progressive disease which wastes the muscles or takes the memory, or a terminal cancer in a loved one, or a bereavement where our 'Isaac' has to be given up to God. At such times faith may come near to breaking point. 'Where was God when my son died?' cried a mother in despair to her pastor. 'Where he was when his own Son died,' was the quiet reply.

For us all and in all the changing scenes of life, he who loves us and is our helper is on the throne *and* in the situation, suffering with us but also leading us to his glory where every tear will be wiped away by our Father in person![10] God is with us in the darkest times and Christ will meet us in these times, placing them among our profoundest spiritual experiences:

> But (when so sad thou can'st not sadder)
> Cry – and upon thy so sore loss
> Shall shine the traffic of Jacob's ladder
> Pitched betwixt heaven and Charing Cross.
>
> Yea, in the night, my Soul, my daughter
> Cry – clinging heaven by the hems;
> And lo, Christ walking on the water
> Not of Gennesareth, but Thames.[11]

Meantime, sufferings remain and are a test for us all at

some time or other. And it is a sobering fact of pastoral experience that troubles will usually drive the nominal believer *from* God and the true believer *to* God.

Sometimes the greatest test in a believer's life may be in *prosperity, success, even riches*. I have known people who were doing well until these things came and spoiled them! We all know the fable about the elements who competed to get a traveller's coat off his back. Wind, rain and snow all tried and failed, for he only wrapped the coat more tightly around him. But when the sun shone he was glad to take it off in the warmth, and the sun won. So we fatally relax in prosperity, or become proud and overbearing in success, or foolishly choose the toys of life when rich and miss its opportunities to do serious good.

Sometimes God's best decision is to say 'No' to our requests, to lead us away from the goals we set ourselves, even to disappoint our expectations – and all in answer to our daily prayer 'Lead us not into temptation'. We do well to make our goal the *character* which is the priority of the wise man in Proverbs 30. He knows that temptation can take many forms and he knows his vulnerability on more than one side:

> Two things I ask of you, O Lord;
>   do not refuse me before I die:
> Keep falsehood and lies far from me;
>   give me neither poverty nor riches,
>   but give me only my daily bread.
> Otherwise, I may have too much and disown you
>   and say, 'Who is the Lord?'
> Or I may become poor and steal
>   and so dishonour the name of my God.[12]

At first it may seem strange, in the light of all this, that we should be told to pray that God will not test us, when it is sometimes his way to do so.[13] But the sense of the petition may well be 'Do not test us beyond our strength', and it may be so here as a way of confessing to our Father that, in a world of fierce conflict and many dangers, we feel

162

very vulnerable and ill-equipped, and feel too the poverty of our faith and love. This is our way of leaning on 'the everlasting arms'.[14]

Notes

1 Jer. 31:33.
2 Gen. 22:1–2.
3 Deut. 8:1–5, 16–18.
4 Judg. 2:20–3.
5 Amos 3:2.
6 Ps. 119:67, 71, 72.
7 e.g. Rom. 5:3–5; Heb. 12:4–13; 1 Pet. 1:6–9.
8 2 Tim. 2:3.
9 Job 23:10; 2 Cor. 6:3–10.
10 Rev. 21:4.
11 Francis Thompson, 'The Kingdom of God', *Works*, vol. II, London, Burns & Oates, n.d., pp. 226–7.
12 Prov. 30:7–9.
13 Jas. 1:2–4.
14 Deut. 33:27.

TEMPTATION AS SEDUCTION

Satan – now why bring him into this? Who needs an out-dated mythology to help them maintain a modern morality? Who really needs this part of the prayer? Well, I do for one and you do for another. A prayer against temptation which did not include the tempter would be short-sighted, to say the least, and probably short-lived too. Nothing guarantees defeat more than underestimating the enemy, and a Satan relegated to fairyland is an adversary underestimated with a vengeance.

But can we really believe in a personal devil or demons in this modern world? Is such a belief not primitive in the extreme? Are such concepts relevant or even coherent to men and women in our society? These are forceful questions and they are often forcefully put. However, the Christian believer must not be bullied into silence by incredulity touched with scorn.

Those who dismiss this belief usually dismiss not only Satan but God, not only the demonic but the whole realm of the supernatural. Indeed, that is their problem: they see this world and the physical universe as a closed system where everything can be adequately explained in purely natural terms. They have no room in their world-view for Christian belief as a whole or for this as a part of the Christian's world-view. They have no room for God, for Jesus Christ as the Son God sent into the world, for the need of salvation or the good news that men and women can be reconciled to God through Jesus Christ.

They are at a polar remove from their ancestors, who went in dread of evil spirits every day, who saw them behind every tree and in every event and who sought to charm or bribe them lest they were possessed or slain by them. These descendants have, if I might change the image, moved from the tropics to the ice-cap, from a world over-peopled with spirits to a bleak and icy world where humanity lives alone, dug in against the cold of its own hopelessness, without God or a gospel that rises above death and opens a way beyond it.

C.S. Lewis writes:

> There are two equal and opposite errors into which our race can fall, about the devils. One is to disbelieve in their existence. The other is to believe and to feel an excessive and unhealthy interest in them. They themselves are equally pleased by both errors and hail a materialist or a magician with the same delight.[1]

We ignore Scripture if we ignore this matter. We do not find in Scripture either 'an excessive and unhealthy interest' in or an unreal avoidance of the matter. The Old Testament tells us of the temptation of Eve, the testing of Job and the accusation of Joshua,[2] and it recognises the reality of demonic presence and activity in the world[3] especially, perhaps, in the worship of false gods. Jesus clearly believed in the existence of Satan as a personal and distinct being and told his followers of one encounter of particular force which he experienced after his baptism.

In the gospels we find many explicit references to Satan and his power in the earth, but also the clear announcement that the kingdom of God has come in with Jesus's ministry, and that, as light drives darkness back, so Christ in his kingdom-activity will rob Satan of his possessions, bringing men and women to freedom as the gospel of the kingdom spreads throughout the earth. Deliverance from the evil one took various forms, ranging from exorcism through certain healings and on to the preaching of the gospel.[4]

Today as ever, and in our land as in any, Satan continues his work, encouraging rebellion against God,[5] blinding men and women to the truth of the gospel,[6] lulling some to sleep[7] and engulfing others in violence,[8] and the cry goes up from believers who are not exempt from Satan's cunning, deceit and malice: 'Deliver us from the evil one'.

Such a prayer, however, need not be the dying gasp of a drowning man but the daily recognition that 'The reason the Son of God was revealed was that he might destroy the works of the evil one'.[9] In that confidence we may face temptation and opposition and all danger. We do not know ourselves or our situation if we imagine that we do not need this prayer or its warning. We like to think that we are very reasonable, sensible, self-controlled and self-determining beings. Yet for all this we are complex and contradictory creatures. Our attitudes are often formed and affected subconsciously, by forces and influences of which we are only dimly aware. Our behaviour is much affected by external pressures, influences, limitations etc., and many forces in society 'pull our strings'. We are neither as free nor as fine as we like to think. Dr. D. M. Lloyd-Jones has this to say:

> The fatal mistake made constantly about man is to regard him only as a mind or an intellect; and therefore the whole basis of secular teaching is that all you need to do is to tell men about the evil nature of certain things . . . Conversely, if you tell them to do certain things because they are right and good and true and noble, they will jump at them and do them. What ignorance of human nature! . . . They will not see that man in the main is irrational . . . a kind of iceberg – two-thirds out of sight in the depth, in the darkness . . . man is not governed by his mind, his intellect, his understanding, but by his desires, impulses, and instincts, by what the psychologists call 'drives'.[10]

And it is here in particular that Satan is very active, for evil is in its own nature very irrational, incoherent, inconsistent and elusive. Reason is for Satan a weapon, a means to an end, a way to manipulate a situation. But it is also dispensable, disposable, and can easily be circumvented. Often we ourselves use our intellects in the service of our prejudices, our passions and our lusts, which have been encouraged or enticed by Satan. Michael Green cites a striking example of this:

> Aldous Huxley with rare honesty and candour admits that he was unwilling to commit himself to the demands of Christian discipleship. In a passage in *Ends and Means* he writes: 'I had motives for not wanting the world to have a meaning; consequently assumed that it had none, and was able without any difficulty to find satisfying reasons for this assumption . . . For myself, the philosophy of meaninglessness was essentially an instrument of liberation, sexual and political.'[11]

It is clear from Scripture that Satan's great hatred is for God; his great desire is to oppose, dishonour and defeat God and having been cast from heaven he continues that warfare on earth, seeking the corruption and destruction of the unique race God made to share his eternity. In particular, he seeks to corrupt, divert or destroy the Church of God on earth, the one agency which exists to reclaim a lost world and to save men and women. His malice and subtlety are particularly directed against the people of God in all ages. Because of that he is called 'the accuser of the brethren' – though I hasten to add that he is not gender specific in his accusations! He is out to accuse us before God and other people, to mock God and to discredit us. He even accuses us to ourselves: taking away shame when he tempts us and then piling it on when we give in, so that we are ashamed even to come to God for forgiveness.

Let me take you briefly through some of the stages of seduction, the steps of temptation to evil, which Satan employs.

First, he presents the temptation in its most attractive form, however ugly the reality. Like an angler, he presents the bait and hides the hook: he shows us the enjoyment or the profit of the wrong-doing and hides the later guilt and shame and hurt which we shall feel. The only way to be safe here is to keep away from the bait as well as the hook! It may be wrong company, a wrong relationship, a wrong book or film, a step in the wrong direction in career advancement. You cannot pray 'Lead us not into temptation' if you lead yourself into temptation!

Second, he persuades. First he presents, then he persuades. He cannot force you into sin but he can talk you into sin, engaging you in a fascinating conversation on the rights and wrongs of it all. And he is an expert in debate – especially on ethics! He can argue things on to their heads, calling evil good and good evil and supporting it by a series of seemingly watertight arguments.[12] He will tell you to be yourself when he is only taking you further and further from your true self. He will talk of self-fulfilment even as he leads you to self-disintegration. He will imply that you can join the rat race without becoming one of the rats. He will persuade you not to be ashamed to sin – only ashamed to repent and return to God.

Third, he persists. One swallow doesn't make a summer and one victory doesn't win a war; neither does one self-denying decision for God mean the end of the matter. Ours is a spiritual warfare which lasts as long as life in this battlefield world lasts. Satan has no sense of honour or fair dealing, and he will follow us through a life of service to Christ and into old age, still tempting, persisting, sowing doubts and fears in our weakest, most vulnerable hours.

Hence we see the solemn need for Christians to develop their spiritual life. If there is consistent attack and erosion in one or two sensitive areas in our lives, we must be on guard and daily praying and seeking strength in precisely those areas.

Fourth, he pressurises. In his famous passage on the believer taking 'the whole armour of God' to withstand

Satan's attacks, Paul speaks of 'the evil day'. And whatever else that 'evil day'[13] may mean, it is a fact of Christian experience that you will encounter days of special pressure, significant temptation, when evil comes in like a flood.

At such times our cry to God will be strongest, but so will be his protection if we trust in him and strive with him against the pressures of the hour. He has promised he 'will not let you be tempted beyond what you can bear. But when you are tempted, he will also provide a way out so that you can stand up under it.'[14] However, it is surprising what we can bear with God's help, and the trial may be both long and hard. Such times are not to be lightly regarded: we cannot say, in foolish, vain confidence, 'I'll never fall', 'I can take it'. Better to know our own weakness and pray daily: 'Lead us not into temptation, but deliver us from the evil one'.

Let Paul's words be our wisdom and our warning: 'For our struggle is not against flesh and blood, but against . . . the spiritual forces of evil in the heavenly realms . . . with this in mind, be alert and always keep on praying for all the saints.'[15] In the following two sections we will study two common areas of temptation – the intellectual life and the moral life – and two specific temptations within those areas.

Notes

1 C.S. Lewis, *The Screwtape letters* London, Godfrey Bles, 1942, preface.
2 Gen. 3:1–5; Job 1:6–12; Zech. 3:1–2.
3 e.g. 1 Sam. 16:15ff.; 1 Kgs. 22:21–3.
4 e.g. Luke 10:17–20; 11:14–22; 13:16.
5 Eph. 2:1–3.
6 2 Cor. 4:3–4.
7 1 John 5:19.
8 1 Pet. 5:8–9.
9 1 John 3:8(AV).

10 D.M. Lloyd-Jones, *The Christian warfare*, Edinburgh, The Banner of Truth Trust, 1976, p. 29.

11 Michael Green, *World on the run*, Leicester, IVP, 1983, p. 32.

12 Gen. 3:1, 4–5; Isa. 5:20; Matt. 4:1–11.

13 Eph. 6:13, 'when the day of evil comes'. See the entire passage, vv. 10–20.

14 1 Cor. 10:13.

15 Eph. 6:12, 18.

INTELLECTUAL TEMPTATION: THE TEMPTATION TO DOUBT

Satan's primary and most persistent temptation is the temptation to unbelief and rebellion: opposing God's will with our ambition, his sovereignty with our self-advancement, his glory with our pride. There are many turnings from the road of faith which deviate gradually until we are going in a quite opposite direction. Satan often tempts us not at first to defiance, but to doubts. He tempts us to doubt God's existence on the one hand or God's commitment to us on the other hand, the reality of his threats or the validity of his promises, the wisdom of his laws or the truth of his gospel. Temptation now, as ever, is usually prefaced by 'Did God really say . . .?'[1]

Faith always has to deal with doubts from early youth to late age. Doubt is often waiting round the next corner with the unexpected, or lurking in the undergrowth of a new argument, or curled up in a bad experience, or tracking our footsteps alongside an old problem. Satan never gives up. If he cannot destroy you he will try to disturb you. And he knows that doubts disturb us deeply; they hurt us precisely in proportion to our love for God, our longing for him, our surrender to him. That is why the best of us will be beset with doubts from time to time. A world-famous missionary leader, George Verwer of Operation Mobilisation, said recently to our congregation, 'I've lived my whole life on the edge of agnosticism. So you people who talk of your doubts all the time, look, any idiot can doubt; faith just costs a little bit more.' After thirty years of faithful, fruitful but not peaceful service, he should know! Hence we all need to learn to handle doubts in a mature, stable way: not pretending, not panicking and not pitying ourselves into spiritual depression and vulnerability, but coping with the strong winds of temptation and dealing patiently with the grit that gets into the eyes of faith at times so that we cannot see too well for a while. And this means that it is indeed *faith* that must handle doubt: not fear, not an enforced neutrality, not a helpless complaisance, but faith.

The way to approach your doubts is first to understand your faith. And when I speak of *your* faith I mean *the* faith, that is, the great historic facts and the glorious spiritual realities of the Christian faith. Not, in the first place, your believing, but your beliefs. That way you don't start with the negative and you don't start with yourself! Faith grows strong by looking to God and to what he has done, by listening to God and understanding his will and way.

This was the Psalmist's way in Psalm 73. There he tells us he nearly lost his faith when he saw how the godless prosper.[2] He felt guilty about this but could not shake it off 'till I entered the sanctuary of God; then I understood their final destiny.'[3] Before the massive reality of God the judge of all the earth, and in the perspective of final judgements and ultimate things, he saw how hollow the pride of the unbelieving was[4] and how foolish he had been to quarrel with God.[5] He saw that what mattered supremely in his own experience was that he was loved by God and held in an eternal relationship.[6] The rest could wait God's time, God's hour and God's resolution. So the Psalm begins and ends with statements of triumphant and joyful faith: 'God is good'[7] and 'it is good for me to be near God'.[8] This is faith's 'bottom line'.

We must always be aware that we live our lives, even as Christians, in the world of the Fall. A global catastrophe has distanced our world from God's heaven, wrapped it in silence from the sight or sound of spiritual and supernatural realities. Our world is not normal, and God's dealings with it are not normal. Even with believers, God's dealings are to a very real extent conditioned by sin in the world and in ourselves. Hence while he is the God who speaks[9] he is often silent,[10] while he is the God who is near[11] he is often felt as far away,[12] while he is the God of many mercies[13] we must go through many hardships to inherit the kingdom of God,[14] and while he is the God who heals[15] yet, 'if Christ is in you, the body is dead because of sin [still subject to death, doomed to die], yet your spirit is alive because of righteousness [the righteousness of God[16] that is given by faith].'[17]

If faith is to cope with the world as it is, it must realise that the world as it is is not the world as it was meant to be. It is a damaged world, and ours is a broken humanity, kept in the mercy of God yet reaping the fruit of its own Fall in the judgement of God. God, as Isaiah so beautifully shows in his prophecies,[18] has a wonderful future for our world, a future in which it (and we) will be healed and glorious. Yet in the present so many times we have to say, as he does, 'Truly you are a God who hides himself.'[19]

Doubts come as we look at the shadows, at the apparent absence of God in situations, but faith listens to the promise,[20] looks forward to the reconciliation[21] and rejoices in the light.

For the New Testament believer, the Christian, much more is clear, for while 'the law was given through Moses, grace and truth came through Jesus Christ'.[22] He is the great antidote to doubt, and his stature dwarfs all doubt. So when you are tempted to doubt, start with your objective faith, not your subjective doubts. Is your faith well-founded on the historic reality of Jesus,[23] on the reliability of his claims[24] and on the coherence of his gospel?[25] The way to approach your doubts is to understand your faith: is it reasonable, is it well-founded, is it effective? Often Christians know too little about the faith they profess. They carry a Sunday School faith into a university world, they are experts in their field but amateurs in their faith.

And if your faith is intellectually developed *is it put into practice*, is it an active faith? Doubt is only properly dealt with by faith developed in understanding *and* obedience. Passive intellectual cogitation is not enough. Faith must be put to work; it cannot remain strong and healthy kept only in the inner life: 'My teaching is not my own. It comes from him who sent me. If anyone chooses to do God's will, he will find out whether my teaching comes from God or whether I speak on my own.'[26]

We must distinguish between our doubts on the one hand and our attitude to them on the other. Christian people are often deeply upset by the presence of doubt. They begin to ask, 'If we doubt, does that mean we are not really Christians at all? Does doubting damn us?' The answer to that last question is probably that one kind of doubting does; another kind does not.

If you prefer doubt to belief, if you hide behind your doubts as convenient excuses to keep you from facing God and his call on your life, if you cherish your doubt and side with it – then you show that you are not after all on the side of God, but still running from him, ranged against him and without claim on him. Your doubt in that case is really unbelief and it is unbelief that damns. James' 'double-minded man'[27] is not the true believer, faithful but fighting. He is rather the man who still hasn't decided where his loyalty lies; he is 'unstable in all he does', and his doubt is not a troublesome relic of the old life but a fundamental ambivalence about God.

However, if, quite differently from this, you struggle with doubt in hope and fear, longing to be altogether God's child and hating everything which comes between you and him, including especially doubt and disobedience, then your struggle with doubt is not a sign of unbelief but its opposite! It is a sign of faith. Your very fear is your comfort!

It is not the presence of doubt but the absence of faith which is the damning thing. Faith can and often does coexist with doubt, but it is not equalled by it nor need it be crippled by it. Faith by its very nature is stronger than doubt, as light by its very nature is stronger than darkness. We are 'justified by faith', not by the amount of faith but by the truth of faith. If it leads us to Christ as Saviour and Lord it is saving faith, however small and

174

frail it may be. This is because ultimately it is Christ as the object of faith who saves, not faith in itself, and a strong Saviour can say to a weak faith, 'Daughter/son, your faith has healed you. Go in peace and be freed from your suffering.'[28]

We must get our doubts themselves into proper perspective. When we struggle with doubts, we must not blindly give them a credit they do not deserve. We are inclined to flatter our doubts and to be afraid of them because of a reputation we ourselves have given to them. We often give them a character for honesty and uprightness and intellectual strength that they do not deserve. Often we are fooled into respecting our doubts more than our beliefs, as if our doubts were free of any prejudice, of anything irrational or even of anything mistaken.

The fact is, of course, that your doubts are no bigger or stronger or more formidable than your own little intellect. They are as susceptible to your very un-intellectual sinfulness and weakness and instability as anything else in your life. Often our doubts (which we sometimes run away from instead of facing down) are not nearly as formidable or unanswerable as we think at first. Like some small dogs which set up a furious barking as we pass their gate, making us jump nearly out of our skins, but which beat a hasty retreat when we take a step towards them, so it can be with the doubts we fear to voice and examine: they can be poodles pretending to be alsatians!

What is of supreme importance in this whole matter, whether our doubts are few or many, weak or strong, is what we do with them in relation to Jesus Christ.

Some years ago, a young man from a fine Christian family came to me. He was about to go up to Cambridge to study but knew he was leaving behind a matter which had never been resolved. All his life he had shown great respect for his parents' faith and consistently joined them in church attendance, yet he

himself had not made a profession of faith. 'You see,'
he said to me with a slight smile, 'I can't shelve my
doubts.' I replied, 'No, but I see that you can shelve
your Saviour.' He looked startled but interested, and I
continued, 'You see, something has to be in the centre
of your life and some things have to be on the shelves
– and you've chosen to put Jesus Christ on the shelves.
My point is that he ought to be in the centre and the
doubts on the shelves, but you have exactly reversed
that. Now I want to ask you whether you really believe
that Jesus is small enough to be on the shelf. Personally,
I think *that* ought to be your biggest doubt, and that
you should transfer most of the respect you are giving
to your doubts to him, and that you should put him
in the centre and your doubts on the shelves. Isn't it
time to do that?' I am glad to say that one week later
he made an appointment to see me and tell me that
Jesus was off the shelf and at the centre! You see, it
isn't having doubts but what you do with them that
matters most.

Notes

1 Gen. 3:1.
2 Ps. 73:2, 13–14.
3 Ps. 73:15–16.
4 Ps. 73:18–20.
5 Ps. 73:21–2.
6 Ps. 73:23–6.
7 Ps. 73:1.
8 Ps. 73:28.
9 Ps. 19:1–11.
10 Ps. 28:1.
11 Ps. 23:1–6.
12 Ps. 22:1–2.
13 Jas. 1:17.
14 Acts 14:22.

15 Ps. 103:3; Acts 3:6.
16 Rom. 1:17.
17 Rom. 8:10.
18 e.g. chapters 11, 60–6.
19 Isa. 45:15.
20 John 16:33.
21 Col. 1:20.
22 John 1:17.
23 1 Cor. 15:1–11.
24 John 14:1–10.
25 Rom. 5:1–11.
26 John 7:16–17.
27 Jas. 1:5–8.
28 Mark 5:34.

MORAL TEMPTATION: THE TEMPTATIONS OF OUR SEXUALITY

God's provision

God has made our human race in two genders, male and female.[1] We share his image and dignity which places us above all other created life-forms in this world.[2] We are made for God and each other and are in various ways incomplete without each other.[3] We are not solitary but social creatures and need each other in different ways and at different levels. We need to belong, both in families and in wider groupings: we need friends and we need families, we need partnerships in our working lives and we need partners in our domestic lives. The highest form of partnership is exclusive, life-long union between husband and wife: a union which restores an ancient oneness[4] and which can make possible again an ancient trust, intimacy and acceptance: 'The man and his wife were both naked, and they felt no shame.'[5] We might with justification say that Adam and Eve stood before each other with nothing to hide, open and transparent to one another, mentally and physically. But the text is not to be 'spiritualised', it refers to their sex lives if it refers to anything.

There is a long anti-sexual tradition in the Christian Church, but it is not a biblical one. Genesis tells us that God made us sexual beings from the start. The monastic and ascetic ideals of the early and medieval Church could not cope with that. It misread Paul, elevated celibacy above marriage, regarded sexuality as part of the fallenness of human nature and left a tragic legacy of shame and confusion. As Lewis Smedes put it: 'Augustine could not imagine an innocent person in paradise turned on sexually; a sinless Adam could never have been aroused by a pure Eve: Adam and Eve could not have walked with

God in the day and made spontaneous love at night . . .
This was how Augustine felt about sexuality.'[6]

But this is a far cry from Genesis or the Song of Solomon
or Jesus or Paul. Sex with all its joys was God's idea
before it was ours. Jesus celebrated marriage by his
own presence at weddings,[7] and taught the basis of
gender distinction, the God-givenness of marriage and
the sanctity of sexual union.[8] The apostle Paul was far
from the frigid misogynist of popular myth. He understood
profoundly the psychology of sex,[9] the importance of sex in
marriage[10] and the uniqueness of sexual union in uniting
persons, not only bodies. He even made it an illustration
of the perfect union between Christ the bridegroom and
the Church his bride.[11]

Our distortion

However, the Bible is a thoroughly realistic book. We
are no longer in Eden. Sin has disturbed society in many
ways, including the unique society of husband and wife. It
has brought domination, manipulation and deceit into the
most sacred of human relationships[12] and it has debased
the most profound of its intimacies – sexual union. There
are, in the New Testament, several lists of human sins and
vices.[13] From them we learn several important lessons in
regard to our subject.

**Our sexuality is important to God and our misuse of our
sexuality is a serious sin**. It is clear from the prominence
given to sexual sins – they either head the list or occur
repeatedly during them – that the sexual drive is both
strong and seriously affected by the Fall. Our sexuality
has become badly distorted and is to an extent out of
control. Its satisfaction has become an end in itself, not
an expression of self-giving, faithful love or a precious
part of the process of having children. This matters
greatly to God, not because sex is wrong or forbidden,
but because when distorted or misdirected or abused it
becomes something else, something without the beauty,
truth or meaning of his original gift.

Sexual sins exist alongside other equally serious sins. People

179

'clean' of sexual immorality may be corrupted by greed, distorted with malice, cruel in slander, utterly condemned in arrogance. They may do as much, or more, harm than others they look down on for sexual immorality or promiscuity. They may, in the words of the old couplet:

> Compound for sins they are inclined to
> By damning those they have no mind to.

The seriousness of other sins, however, does not lessen the seriousness of sexual sin.

Sexual misbehaviour is an evil which promotes further evil. Paul in Galatians 5 speaks of 'sexual immorality, impurity and debauchery', and later in the list he adds 'hatred, discord, jealousy, fits of rage'.[14] And it is a fact of life, as we read in our newspapers every day, that much jealousy, bitterness, discord and violence grows out of fornication and adultery. No one lives to themselves, and no one sins to themselves alone either. We never know where sin will end. We cannot be permissive in one thing only.

It is against such a background in Scripture that we are able to recognise the powerful forces of moral decay and decadence in our own day, when temptation to sexual sin is more widespread than ever.

We live amidst an extraordinary obsession with sex and sexuality. TV and films, books and magazines are to a striking degree preoccupied with sex and are providing an increasing amount of sexually explicit material which is turning us into a nation of voyeurs. The privacy of sex is invaded because the sacrosanct nature of sex is discarded. Younger children are bombarded with reports or images of behaviour which they cannot emotionally understand, teenagers have passions excited which they cannot satisfy with marital sex and are increasingly seduced into pre-marital sex, older people are embarrassed and distressed and parents in families often feel helpless before alien and outside forces which shape their children's views and expectations, but often do not themselves have a sufficient moral basis for their own moral code.

Churches and Christians are not unaffected by a society where sex is marketed so cleverly and so seductively. Our moral standards have become lower too, in the films we see and the books we read and even the lives we lead, and sometimes our children's standards are lower still. Many who enter the churches today, as new converts to Christ, have said confessions of sexual abuse, promiscuity, pornography and marriage breakdown through unfaithfulness, and sadly not a few Christian lives and their witness over many years are being ruined by surrender to sexual temptations.

The Christian response

In *The Snare*, an outstandingly perceptive and practically helpful book on sexual temptation, Lois Mowday writes:

> Romans 12:2 says 'Do not conform any longer to the pattern of this world but be transformed by the renewing of your mind'. It's getting tougher and tougher to have a Romans 12 mind-set when we live in a Romans 1 world: 'God . . . gave them over to a depraved mind to do what ought not to be done. They have become fitted with every kind of wickedness, evil, greed and depravity.' (Rom. 1:28–9)[15]

If we are to be transformed by the renewing of our minds then those minds will have to be filled with better thoughts, better images and better standards than we see in the world around. We might do well to place on our TV sets the words of the apostle Paul to a church of young converts who also lived in a permissive society: 'Whatever is true, whatever is noble, whatever is right, whatever is pure, whatever is lovely, whatever is admirable – if anything is excellent or praiseworthy – think about such things . . . And the God of peace will be with you.'[16]

Sexual sin begins in the mind, with a look and a thought that are welcomed and cherished when they ought to be rejected and loathed. People involved in wrong sexual relationships often say and feel that the temptation was too strong for them, that the attraction was just too great, even that the love was too real. But in fact there was a time in its early stages when the temptation could have been dealt with quite easily, when the attraction could have been countered, the occasions of it denied. It is at that much earlier point, when conscious decisions are made in small things, that a line is crossed and a process gets under way that gets out of control. The cry 'It's gone too far, the feelings are too strong, I can't help it any more' is not only a cry of helplessness but a confession of guilt – guilt belonging to an earlier point. The critical sin was committed long before the open sin. Lois Mowday argues that 'immorality is a process' and warns: 'any of us could be in the process right now',[17] free of open sin, clear of gross sin, but unexpectedly, dangerously, near the top of the slippery slope:

> So, if you think you are standing firm, be careful that you don't fall! No temptation has seized you except what is common to man. And God is faithful; he will not let you be tempted beyond what you can bear. But when you are tempted, he will also provide a way out so that you can stand up under it.[18]

The way out may be the direction in which you look – or stop looking (Billy Graham said, 'You can't help the first look, you can help the second!'). The way out may be avoiding company at work or church which part of you enjoys too much. The way out may be an early conversation with your wife or husband, who can help decisively in dealing with unwanted attentions and with early (and still harmless) attractions. The way out may well be a greater care to develop the attractions and intimacies of your own married life.[19] But a way out there always is – and at the end of it a wise and good Father who comforts us, encourages us and leads us on.

Notes

1 Gen. 1:27.
2 Gen. 1:28.
3 Gen. 2:18.
4 Gen. 2:22–4.
5 Gen. 2:25.
6 Lewis Smedes, *Sex and the real world*, Tring, Lion, 1976, p. 13.
7 John 2:1–2.
8 Matt. 19:4–6.
9 1 Cor. 6:16.
10 1 Cor. 7:3–5.
11 Eph. 5:32.
12 Gen. 3:16.
13 e.g. Mark 7:20–3; Gal. 5:19–21; 1 Cor. 6:9–11.
14 Gal. 5:19, 20.
15 Lois Mowday, *The Snare*, Reading, Navpress, 1988, p. 90.
16 Phil. 4:8–9.
17 Lois Mowday, p. 84.
18 1 Cor. 10:12–13.
19 Read carefully Prov. 4:14–23; 1 Cor. 7:1–9.

41

TARGETS OF TEMPTATION

We are all targets of temptation, yet there are certain times in our lives, and particular situations, in which we can experience very strong assaults from the enemy.

The new Christian is vulnerable in many respects. Their faith is so new, so young, so weak perhaps, that they may be hardly sure that they *are* Christians and that they have real faith. Doubts may come from unexpected directions and they may be unsure how to handle them, thinking that their very presence argues the absence of true faith. They may be, as yet, hardly aware of the demands of discipleship or the implications of compromise. It may be a shock and a disappointment to discover that things long-cherished may have to be cleared out if their life is to be cleaned up, that life-styles have to alter, maybe in dramatic ways, that a comfortable privacy has to be opened up to others as well as to God, that indifference has to give way to concern and to involvements which are sometimes costly. They may be surprised by the enemy into thinking that their new state or their delightful Christian experiences have put them beyond the reach of temptation. But they will learn that the pendulum of human emotion can swing from the sublime to the sinful in a very short space of time.[1] The new Christian may be, as yet, unfamiliar with the Christian armoury – the weapons of prayer, Scripture, the counsel of older believers, the teaching of experienced preachers etc. They may repeat in their own Christian lives the pattern of Jesus's experience: after his baptism in the Jordan he faced his temptation in the wilderness. So for the new believer all that joy and peace, all the new discoveries of faith in the gospel, all sense of its truth and its relevance, may be challenged in the first weeks. The waters of Jordan soon evaporate in the deserts of Judea; the atmosphere of

Sunday can soon be dispersed on Monday. Consequently they have to learn to walk by faith, not by feelings, storing up in mind and heart the word of God, the sure promises of Christ and the perspectives of Scripture. They have to meet the demands of the day in prayer and its challenges in the Spirit of Christ. They need to be with other Christians frequently for mutual strengthening and encouragement. And these needs are most urgent in the early days of faith.

The strategic Christian is also a particular target of temptation. You may be a light in a dark place, the only Christian in the family or at work or in a club. Others know you, others watch you; they have a right to expect more of you than they do of others and they may one day come to you for help they cannot get from others. There are words only you can speak, love only you can give, a gospel only you can share. If Satan can blot your copybook by inconsistencies now, he will. If he can alienate you from others, build up new barriers, sow further misunderstandings, justify and increase prejudice, he will. They do not know it, but you are their only hope under God, and if Satan can blast that to pieces, he will.

You may be a leader of others in your local church or a leader in the making, missionary or evangelist or pastor. If the tempter can get to *you*, he has won a victory not only in your life but in the lives of many others who look up to you as a model and a guide. Consider the warning of that great Puritan evangelist and theologian of the seventeenth century, Richard Baxter:

Take heed to yourselves because the tempter will make his first or sharpest onset on you. He bears *you* the greatest malice who are committed to doing *him* the greatest harm. He knows what a rout he may make among the people if the leaders fall before their eyes . . . You will have his most subtle insinuations and incessant solicitations and violent assaults. As wise and learned as you are take heed lest he outwit you. The Devil is a greater scholar than you and a nimbler controversialist . . . he will play the juggler with you undiscerned and cheat you of your faith or innocency and you shall not know that you have lost it; nay, he will make you believe it is multiplied or increased when it is lost.[2]

Even the old Christian is a particular target of temptation. Sometimes sick and depressed, sometimes lonely and nervous and often assailed by doubts. 'All passion spent', there may be little excitement in the present and some disillusionment with the past. And Satan, 'a liar and the father of lies',[3] will tell you that it was all in vain, all a beautiful dream or a hollow mockery. If ever there was a time to lean your full weight on God, it is now. If ever there was a time to take Jesus Christ at his word ('In my Father's house are many mansions. If it were not so *I* would have told you. Would *I* deceive you with vain hopes?')[4] it is now. If ever there was a time to rest on the foundation *God* has laid, it is now. As one old woman said, 'I often tremble on the Rock but the Rock never trembles under me.' Nothing can reverse a life entrusted into the hands of Christ and nothing can rob him of that life, any more than it can rob us of his life:

> My sheep listen to my voice; I know them, and they follow me. I give them eternal life, and they shall never perish; no one can snatch them out of my hand. My Father, who has given them to me, is greater than all; no one can snatch them out of my Father's hand. I and the Father are one.[5]

The worldly Christian is one person in a category of their own, foolishly making themselves targets of temptation, presuming that God will still keep them from sin. But always remember, you cannot pray 'Lead us not into temptation' if you lead yourself into temptation. There are books you cannot read, films you cannot see, company you cannot keep, thoughts you cannot entertain if you want to stay safe, away from the slippery slope which leads to the cliff edge. If you know you have a weakness in an area, don't test it – you may be tempting God and delighting Satan.

I often tell the story of a wealthy woman who decided she would hire a chauffeur to drive her about. After receiving several replies to her advertisement she interviewed each applicant. They all seemed to be satisfactory, but as the interview ended she asked one final question: 'Tell me, as a matter of interest, *how near to danger could you drive me and still keep me safe*?' 'Oh madam,' said the first easily, 'I could drive you to within an inch of danger and you would be safe.' The second at his interview replied with even more confidence, 'Madam, I could take you to within a hair's breadth of danger and you would be quite safe in my hands.' The third candidate for the job, however, looked mystified and rather shocked by the question. 'Madam,' he responded, 'I couldn't answer such a question as that. *I always drive as far from danger as I possibly can.*' He got the job!

That is the only satisfactory way of living this prayer: stay away from temptation, as far away as you possibly can.

For all of us, young and old, new and experienced believers, temptation is a fact of spiritual life which should not take us unawares.

We often become particular targets of temptation *before or after an especially fruitful or decisive work for God*. Christians in leadership, such as preachers, pastors or evangelists, need to be on their guard at such times. It can lift our spirits and sharpen our awareness to recognise that when we feel particularly embattled and struggling we may be about to enter upon a time of significant advance – and that the enemy knows it! On the other hand, it has been a too-common experience that after a time of spiritual blessing and ministerial fruitfulness we can relax our guard and be overtaken by sudden temptation when we, and others, least expect it. Charles Wesley used to warn about 'the swing of the pendulum' in times of revival and it is a danger in or after any time of high spiritual excitement.

Notes

1 Matt. 16:16–17, 22–3.
2 Richard Baxter (1615–91), *The reformed pastor*, Edinburgh, The Banner of Truth Trust, ch. 1, sect. 2.
3 John 8:44.
4 John 14:2 (NIV, see also RSV).
5 John 10:27–30; cf. Rom. 8:38–9.

42

CHRIST'S WORK FOR US

We live in a world blasted by sin and in a life land-mined with temptation. Each of us as a Christian believer is living his or her own 'pilgrim's progress'. Will we make it? Will we hold on to the end?[1] If it were left to us, our response to that would hardly be a confident 'Yes'. But in fact that 'Yes' has been sounded for us by a victorious Christ[2] and a confident apostle.[3] Our deliverances from sin's powerful attractions and Satan's persuasive temptations, from the devil's subtlety and the world's malice, are the result of the work of Christ for us and the work of the Holy Spirit in us.

We are delivered from evil by the death of Christ for us

We very often hear of the death of our Lord Jesus Christ as delivering us from the *penalty* of sin, but far less often hear of it as delivering us from the *power* of sin. And yet this is a clear New Testament emphasis. Thus Paul writes to the Colossians that God 'has rescued us from the dominion of darkness and brought us into the kingdom of the Son he loves, in whom we have redemption, the forgiveness of sins',[4] and to the Galatians that the Lord Jesus Christ 'gave himself for our sins to rescue us from the present evil age.'[5]

F.F. Bruce writes on these words: 'Paul's "evil age" here is an age dominated by an ethically evil power . . . Those who accept the gospel are thereby delivered from the godless *Zeitgeist* (dominating power, moving spirit).' The atoning death of Christ 'delivers them from the realm where sin is irresistible into the realm where Jesus himself is Lord.'[6]

The same message is repeated in Paul's letter to Titus

where he speaks of the Church waiting for the coming of 'our great God and Saviour, Jesus Christ, who gave himself for us to redeem us from all wickedness and to purify for himself a people that are his very own, eager to do what is good'.[7]

We often use the image of a first-century slave-market to illustrate the meaning of redemption – deliverance by the payment of a price, deliverance by purchase; but Paul in Romans 6 also uses it to illustrate the Christian's freedom from the tyranny of sin. There, sin is pictured as a slave-owner from whom we have been set free,[8] who has no more rights over us and to whom we have no obligations: 'But now that you have been set free from sin and have become slaves to God, the benefit you reap leads to holiness, and the result is eternal life. For the wages of sin is death, but the gift of God is eternal life in Christ Jesus our Lord.'[9]

Martin Luther used to tell a quaint story to illustrate this. Luther was a vivid and powerful preacher. When asked how he used to deal with temptation, he would reply: 'Well, when the devil comes knocking at my door and asks, "Who lives here?", my divine Master the Lord Jesus goes to the door and says, "Martin Luther used to live here but he has moved out. Now I am the master of the house."'

We are delivered from evil by the prayers of Christ for us
It is the death of Jesus which *achieves* our salvation but it is the risen life, power and prayers of Christ which *apply* that salvation. In that respect there is an ongoing and day-by-day deliverance in our lives: a deliverance from Satan, temptation and sin in particular. Shortly before his Passion and after celebrating the Passover, our Lord predicted the denials of Peter, but he also promised his recovery in faith and life: 'Simon, Simon, Satan has asked to sift you as wheat. But I have prayed for you, Simon, that your faith may not fail. And when you have turned back, strengthen your brothers.'[10]

That the prayer life of Jesus went far beyond his

immediate disciples and even his own time on earth is clear from the insights we are given in John 17 (more aptly called 'The Lord's Prayer' than this of ours!). There, Jesus prays not only for the disciples but also for 'those who will believe in me through their message',[11] the 'other sheep' which he had spoken of once before,[12] who he would bring into the family and fold of God. They would be under many pressures, from their own families, from their society and, above all and in all, from Satan: 'My prayer is not that you take them out of the world but that you protect them from the evil one.'[13]

The writer of Hebrews tells us that he continues to be the praying Christ in heaven, since as the risen Christ he has 'a permanent priesthood' and connects his prayers with our safety, his intercession in heaven with our assurance of heaven: 'Therefore he is able to save completely those who come to God through him, because he always lives to intercede for them.'[14] Thus the praying Church on earth is connected to the praying Christ in heaven, the Church militant with the Christ potent, the Church struggling with the Christ reigning, the Church in the storm with the Christ on the throne.

I once read of an old Victorian picture which illustrated this in a striking way. The artist had painted a famous gospel scene, the storm on the lake of Galilee, in which Jesus comes to the terrified disciples, walking on the water. However, he had depicted the scene at an earlier stage, and at first all the observer could see was the lashing rain and the heaving waves of the storm-tossed lake, and the frightened disciples desperately rowing their threatened boat in the foreground. Only after a more careful examination could one see a human figure kneeling in prayer among the rocks of the hills bordering the lake. The message? Christ praying in the mountain while the disciples struggled in the storm. It is the perfect illustration of what is happening throughout history where his people are struggling: wrestling with the world, the flesh and the devil. He says to us, as he said to Peter, 'I have prayed for you, that your faith might not fail.' So our prayers meet his prayers; we are not unheard and we are not alone, and we will not be given up to the storm.

Notes

1 Matt. 10:22; 2 Pet. 1:10.
2 John 10:27–8.
3 Phil. 1:6.
4 Col. 1:13–14.
5 Gal. 1:4.
6 F.F. Bruce, *The Epistle of Paul to the Galatians*, Carlisle, Paternoster Press, 1982, pp. 75, 76.
7 Titus 2:14.
8 Rom. 6:12, 14, 17–18, 20.
9 Rom. 6:22–3.
10 Luke 22:31.
11 John 17:20.
12 John 10:16.
13 John 17:15; see also Matt. 10:22,34; John 15:18–21.
14 Heb. 7:25.

THE SPIRIT'S WORK IN US

We are delivered from evil by the Holy Spirit of Christ in us

The Holy Spirit's great desire and work is to make us like Christ, who is like God. It has been God's plan from the beginning that his chosen people (us!) might be 'conformed to the likeness of his Son, that he might be the firstborn among many brothers'.[1] As an indwelling Spirit he has taken up his place at the centre of our being and from that centre he exercises and extends his control,[2] isolating and attacking the sins that threaten us,[3] encouraging us by testifying with our spirits that we are God's children on the way to God's glory,[4] helping us in our weakness and praying with us, our advocate and intercessor on earth as Christ is our advocate and intercessor in heaven.[5] It is thus that our Father in heaven takes us up into his purposes and into his life.[6]

The prayer life of the Christian, like an outcrop of rock on a green hillside, exposes the character and foundation of our lives. These lives of ours, so fragile, so vulnerable, so weak and unsatisfactory where the things of God are concerned, are, notwithstanding, lives which contain a great power, lives which are built upon a mighty foundation, lives which themselves have an eternal significance. Ours are lives which God has claimed as his own;[7] our hearts are the place where Christ is being formed in us, 'the hope of glory';[8] our prayers are the oxygen of heaven which we often need to breathe in the smoke and pollution of earth.

In that pollution many things flourish and grow which are inimical to the Christian life, and we are endangered by them. Hence our Lord, himself wrestling with great temptation in Gethsemane and seeing his disciples unaware and so more vulnerable, warns them, 'Watch and pray so that you will not fall into temptation.'[9] The Holy Spirit makes our prayer life a poisonous atmosphere for Satan and a disinfectant for sin. Sin and prayer cannot live together; each is death to the other. As an old Puritan preacher put it: 'Either praying will make you leave off sinning or sinning will make you leave off praying.'[10] Thus when the apostle Paul is describing the Christian warfare and its armour, he ends his list of weapons with prayer: 'And pray in the Spirit . . . with all kinds of prayers and requests. With this in mind . . . keep on praying for all the saints.'[11]

The Holy Spirit works with similar effect when we read Holy Scripture. He makes the Word of God to be not only information but inspiration and power as we read it.[12] It enlarges our perspective, encourages our resolve, strengthens our faith. Even as we read, the words often come with a certain power and conviction into our minds and hearts. Again it is the Spirit working, working with the Word he inspired in the first place; for he first gave it for people like you and me, and for you and me among them! It is *our* book – his and ours – a letter from home, in which our heavenly Father keeps in touch with us in our earthly travels and trials. It is the history of his mighty acts in our world, the record of the grand redemption achieved by the Son he sent into our world. It is the sound of his voice in our world today, penetrating the static of conflicting philosophies and rising above the chorus of contradictory claims.

As 'the sword of the Spirit',[13] it is still an essential part of 'the full armour of God' with which we can 'take our stand against the devil's schemes'.[14] It compels us to examine ourselves, our lives, their effect, our very motives,[15] and it does so 'so that no one will fall' on their way to God's rest.[16] In a world of temptation to sin, of pressure to conform, of many opportunities but few securities, the believer needs a sure word to guide and to warn. Susannah Wesley, mother of John Wesley, gave her son a Bible to take with him to Oxford and his studies there. The university was not known for high words or great piety; John's brother, Charles, was to write of it after his own studies there as a place 'where learning keeps its loftiest seat and hell its firmest throne!' Knowing that the great university was the graveyard of many a young man's faith and morality, Susannah wrote in the fly-leaf: 'Sin will keep you from this Book; but this Book will keep you from sin.'

The Holy Spirit is not only at work in us; by the same token he is at work in the believers around us, and they are a main part of our protection and comfort when hard times come. Christ not only draws people to himself in every age, he also gathers us together in communities. The New Testament places great emphasis on the Church as the purchased people of God, and not only on the universal Church but on the local church: the believing community in covenant with God and one another. Christ has given the Holy Spirit to the churches to equip them with his gifts and graces, not only for witness in the world but for mutual encouragement and up-building in faith and holiness. The New Testament does not see us growing mature in Christ in isolation but in community, in the fellowship of the Holy Spirit.[17] Thus, for instance, Paul tells the Colossians: 'Let the word of Christ dwell in you richly as you teach and admonish one another with all wisdom, and as you sing psalms, hymns and spiritual songs with gratitude in your hearts to God.'[18]

The Spirit makes the churches of Christ communities of faith and love and help: caring communities in a world too preoccupied, too suspicious, too defensive to care; communities which stimulate and develop faith in a world which devolves and discourages it; communities defined by Christ, headed by Christ and modelled on Christ.

Here we carry one another's burdens[19] and surround one another in the protection of prayer and the encouragement of friendship. Here we meet the grace of God in one another and serve one another in the exercise of his gifts to us.[20] Here we surround each other in the atmosphere of true spiritual worship and counsel one another in the wisdom God gives generously and to all. Here we see in the sacraments and sing in the songs and hear in the preaching the great realities which have gripped us, the mighty love which has found us and the blood-bought right of Jesus to be our Lord and King, our saviour and our guide. It is *together* we can become strong and wise without thereby becoming conceited and hard.[21] It is *together* our light shines out into the world, bright and warm. It is *together* we can resist and defeat Satan, our great enemy. He might easily pick us off one by one in solitariness but not in 'the fellowship of kindred minds'. And in the last great day, when Christ our champion comes to vindicate his waiting Church,[22] then *together* the God of peace will crush Satan under our feet.[23]

Notes

1 Rom. 8:29.
2 Rom. 8:9.
3 Rom. 8:13.
4 Rom. 8:16.
5 Rom. 8:26.
6 Rom. 8:26–7.
7 Isa. 57:15.
8 Col. 1:27, cf. Gal. 4:19.
9 Mark 14:38.
10 Thomas Brooks (1608–80), 'The Privy Key of Heaven' in The Works of Thomas Brooks, Edinburgh, Baner of Truth Trust, 1980, vol. 11.
11 Eph. 6:18.
12 2 Tim. 3:16–17.
13 Eph. 6:17.
14 Eph. 6:11.
15 Heb. 4:12–13.
16 Heb. 4:1–2.
17 1 Cor. 12:7; 2 Cor. 13:14.
18 Col. 3:16.

19 Gal. 6:1–2.
20 Rom. 12:3–8; 1 Pet. 4:7–11.
21 Rom. 12:3, 9–16.
22 1 Thess. 4:13–18; 2 Thess. 2:1–12; Rev. 12:10–12.
23 Rom. 16:20; 1 Cor. 6:2–3.

VI. FOR YOURS IS THE KINGDOM AND THE POWER AND THE GLORY FOR EVER. AMEN

YOURS IS THE KINGDOM
AND THE POWER AND THE GLORY
FOR EVER. AMEN

It is true that this last phrase may not have been an original part of the prayer as Jesus gave it. Scholars generally agree that the manuscript tradition is weighted in favour of omission. Yet it is equally clear that the Church from very early times has added it and used it in her prayers and liturgies.[1] Its parts are taken from various Old Testament texts and are wholly suitable to this New Testament prayer.[2] It is, therefore, an addition which tells us something reliable about God and also something typical about the people who pray the prayer that Jesus gave them.

This is a prayer which ends in praise. The Church's final statement is adoration, pure and simple. She gives herself up to doxology; the struggles of faith, the trials of hope, the losses and the gains of life all take second place to this. It is the true worshipper's final resting place. Yet in this too we express the three greatest and most abiding things: faith, hope and love. For the people of God will always be a people of praise.

Yours is the kingdom

Some years ago I was asked to preach at the opening of a new church in Doncaster. Because the numbers coming were too great to be accommodated in the church complex, the centre of Doncaster Museum was hired for the opening service. Doncaster was an important garrison town in the days of the Roman occupation of Britain and the large and very fine museum there houses many relics of those days. The museum also has a large open area in the centre which is used for public meetings, as it was on this occasion.

I still vividly remember coming to the front of the

congregation to preach the sermon. As I looked out on the scene around me: *there* were the armour, the standards and the weaponry of the Roman legions and the signs of Roman pomp and glory *in glass cases*! And *here* were the once-despised Christians, the spiritual descendants of the martyrs of the arena, singing with joy and confidence the praises of our God and his Christ. Caesar was nothing, the legionaries of the great Roman Empire were nothing, they were dead figures of a dead past; but Jesus Christ was alive and powerfully at work in the world, gathering his people into an eternal kingdom and glory:

> So be it, Lord; Thy throne shall never,
> Like earth's proud empires, pass away;
> Thy kingdom stands and grows for ever,
> Till all Thy creatures own Thy sway.[3]

To be part of that kingdom is a greater privilege than the Caesars of yesterday or Presidents and Prime Ministers of today can ever bestow. Only the reigning Christ who will judge the world will have the power to say, of the kingdom in its full glory, to those who have followed him: 'Come, you who are blessed by my Father; take your inheritance, the kingdom prepared for you since the creation of the world.'[4] To have a place in this kingdom is a privilege as endless as it is incomparable, for 'the righteous will shine like the sun in the kingdom of their Father'.[5]

Yours is the power

We know something of power these days. Astronomers tell us that our sun is 500 times the mass of our earth and is like a vast hydrogen bomb burning slowly. Every second, four million tons of hydrogen are destroyed in explosions near the core. There, at the core, the heat is so intense that a pinhead of material would give off enough heat to kill a human being a million miles away. In one second it emits more energy than man has used up from the earth's resources since history began. Yet all of that is less than the striking of a match to the power of the God we know and love and serve. The colossal energies of the Big Bang and the expanding universe are no adequate measure of his power; they are but the overflow of his reserves, 'the outskirts of his ways'.

The power extolled here, however, is not the power that sustains creation but the power that directs it to a prepared end. It is God's sovereignty in providence and in grace which is the bedrock of biblical religion and the immovable foundation of faith.[6]

Often that power is a hidden power, forging a path through confusion, darkness and storm in a fallen, godless world, choosing the weak things of the world to shame the strong. It is the power of Christ, who is the power and wisdom of God.[7] In the gospels where the sick are healed and even the dead raised, glimpses of that power are revealed, and glimpses too of the new earth it will create, where every vestige and effect of the Fall will be erased. That same power is at work today even when the body is dead 'because of sin', where sickness defeats us for a while. [8] Even where death by martyrdom comes with no visible rescue, faith sees a Christ who has 'the power of an indestructible life', seated at the right hand of God 'far above all rule and authority, power and dominion', a coming Christ waiting to vindicate our trust. [9]

The last enemy that shall be destroyed is death, even death in the body, for 'Multitudes who sleep in the dust of the earth will awake: some to everlasting life, others to shame and everlasting contempt.' [10] The power that opens the graves on the last day, the power which will raise glorified bodies for the already-glorified souls of believers, is the power of God which raised Christ Jesus our Head. For Christ has been raised from the dead as 'the firstfruits of those who have fallen asleep', and he 'by the power that enables him to bring everything under his control, will transform our lowly bodies so that they will be like his glorious body'. [11] This is the 'incomparably great power' of God which is vested in Jesus Christ and which is already at work in we who believe, so that Paul can give his blessing to the Ephesian Christians in these words: 'Now to him who is able to do immeasurably more than all we ask or imagine, according to his power that is at work within us, to him be glory in the church and in Christ Jesus throughout all generations, for ever and ever! Amen.' [12]

Yours is the glory

You and I gasp at the glory of a sunset, marvel at the structure of a crystal, absorb the wonder of a landscape and have a sense of glory from what is created. Or perhaps we hear a symphony or a sonata, see a painting or read out a poem, and have a sense of glory in what we ourselves create from the structures of sound, the sight of colours in God's world or the sense of occasion in human life. Take all these things and multiply their beauty or their brilliance, their depth of complexity or their height of perfection a thousand million times, and we will still have only a faint sense of the glory of God. For if there is all this beauty outside God, how much beauty there must be in the being of God:

> O worship the Lord in the beauty of holiness!
> Bow down before him, his glory proclaim.[13]

In the Old Testament, the glory of God appeared in a quite special way as an aura of dazzling light: it was called the *Kabod Yahweh*, the glory of God. Those that saw it could hardly describe it, and it left them feeling utterly weak and overawed and even prostrate.[14] Such a demonstration of glory was meant to show the utter incomparability of God not only in majesty but also in purity, not only in power but also in goodness and righteousness and justice.[15] His glory must not be given to any other being or power in the universe. He alone is God, and there is and will be no other.[16]

It is all the more startling, therefore, to find throughout the New Testament the honours of Yahweh shared with Jesus in forgiving sins, in judging the world, in receiving the honours and worship due to God, and the name which is divine.[17] Moreover, Jesus himself is described in terms of his pre-existent life in the Godhead as 'the radiance of God's glory'; in the words of one of the Church's greatest confessions he is and ever was:

> God of God,
> Light of Light,
> true God of true God,
> begotten not made,
> of one substance with the Father.[18]

In his earthly life, the incarnate Son lived for the glory of God; in his exalted life, the glorified Son shares the glory of God. Now the kingdom is his and the power is his and the glory is his. It is a glory which he can share uniquely because he enjoyed equal glory with the Father before the world began.[19] It is a glory which Saul of Tarsus saw streaming as dazzling light from the face of the Nazarene and knew they had crucified the Lord of glory.[20]

Yet into the blessing of that glory we are called: for, as much as we creatures can do, we too shall share the glory which Christ has purchased for us by his death and holds for us in his endless resurrection life.[21] So Paul urges the Thessalonians and us 'to live lives worthy of God, who calls you into his kingdom and glory'.[22]

For almost 2,000 years the followers of Christ have repeated this prayer and have sealed it with this final statement. In the mouths of believers everywhere and in all conditions, it has expressed the presence of the great triad: faith, hope and love.[23] It has been a statement of faith, an expression of hope and a declaration of love, and with these three things we end our study of this prayer.

A statement of faith

What is faith? It is not easy to define faith as such. It is hard for faith to explain itself. This is not at all surprising, for the content of faith is its object and not itself; the thing believed rather than the act of believing. Ask us, then, to speak of God our Father and of his grace in Jesus Christ, and we shall speak freely and without embarrassment. But do not ask us to speak much on 'faith' or 'our faith' in the abstract, for we have no faith abstracted from him in whom we have faith.

Faith finds no great quality or virtue in itself but in its object, God: his existence, his character, his word, his mighty acts in the biblical history, and now, above all, in his only Son our Lord Jesus Christ, incarnate, crucified, risen and exalted. This is the way faith lives, not striving to will something into existence but resting on something God has brought into existence: his kingdom, his power, his glory made known to us and shared with us in the gospel of Jesus Christ. Faith then is *believing God*, recognising and receiving his revelation of himself and his truth and committing ourselves to him for this life and the next, for time and eternity.

Faith, true faith, saving faith, has specific content. It is neither mysticism nor gullibility nor a generous open-mindedness. As John Stott puts it, 'Faith is not a synonym for credulity or superstition . . . Faith is a reasonable trust.'[24] It is based on the historic events of the gospel, not on a supra-historical mythology or a cloudy supernaturalism. Above all, it is based upon the reliability of Jesus: his claims, his offer of forgiveness and his promise of eternal life. It is through him that we enter the kingdom of God, it is he who is the power of God for salvation and it is by him that we will enter the glory of the Father's house.

It is faith's triumph that in a world of contradiction and contention it can look to the God and Father of our Lord Jesus Christ and say, 'yours is the kingdom and the power and the glory for ever. Amen.'

An expression of hope

The doxology at the end of the Lord's Prayer leaves us looking upward and also looking forward to a God of undefeatable purpose, of unequalled power and eternal glory. It is a final note of defiance to the forces of darkness and of confidence in the God who is Light, who is above all and over all, blessed for ever.[25] The biblical word for such confidence is *hope*. In common use today, hope is a synonym for uncertainty, as in the statement: 'We hope for good weather during our holidays.' In the New Testament use of the word, however, hope has a quite different meaning. It signifies confident expectation, strong assurance, and it is never tinged with nervousness or alarm, as so often in secular contexts.

The character and dominance of hope was a striking feature of early Christian faith in contrast to much philosophy and religious thought. One scholar writes: 'Living hope as a fundamental religious attitude was unknown in Greek culture . . . In the final analysis men had to stand without hope before the hostile forces of guilt and death.'[26] We see much of that today, too, and it has been a very dominant feature of much popular post-war philosophy, leading to cynicism and despair. Saul Bellow writes graphically of this in the novel *Herzog*: 'This generation thinks – and this is its thoughts – that nothing faithful, vulnerable, fragile can be durable or have any true power. Death waits for these things as a cement floor waits for a dropping light bulb.'[27]

As a typical Woody Allen line puts it, 'The future is not what it used to be.' But that is just what the believer denies as he or she ends prayer with such words as these. The future is still *precisely* what it used to be, because God is unchanging in his character, purposes, promises and power: 'I the Lord do not change. So you, O descendants of Jacob, are not destroyed'; and because 'Jesus Christ is the same yesterday and today and for ever.'[28]

Christ has come, Christ has died, Christ is risen, Christ is coming again:

> . . . and therein lies all hope on the Christian view. For hope is not a mere refusal to accept defeat, a heroic virtue to be mustered and maintained by noble souls in the face of suffering, disaster, despair, or even of life's mere drudgery. Much less is it an attitude of general optimism to be cultivated from, by and for

itself. It is the response of joy that flashes to life in anyone who sees what Christ's coming means, like the thrill that comes to haggard clumps of war prisoners who see the camp gates suddenly crashing inward and their own troops arriving. [29]

It is with such hope that faith sees that day approaching and a pilgrim church daily affirms, 'yours is the (in-coming) kingdom and the (unfailing) power and the (approaching) glory.'

A declaration of love

The 'amen' at the end of the prayer is a form of an old Hebrew word which indicates certainty and dependability. It was used to confirm a statement made by someone else or as a response which acknowledged the validity and binding nature of an agreement. As such, it is like a personal signature, involving ourselves in what has been said. It could be translated 'so be it' or 'I agree' or 'surely it is so'. Jesus unusually, perhaps uniquely, used it at the beginning rather than the end of some of his sayings to authorise them as certain and reliable, to make them binding on his followers, and as an expression of his own majesty and authority.

In the mouths of God's willing people, however, and in the mouths of his children who pray the Lord's Prayer, the amen is a final note of love and self-giving. For the kingdom is his – and yet he has shared it with us. And the power is his – which might have crushed us but which has caught us, in the ambush of an infinite and everlasting love surrounding us without the possibility of escape from it'. [30] And the glory is his – a glory which might have been for ever forbidden us, leaving us exiled in unending darkness. But with matchless grace and marvellous generosity, he calls us into his glory and makes it the inheritance of all believers.[31] In view of such things, and in view of their cost at Calvary, how can our final amen be anything other than an amen of self-giving love, in response to God's self-giving love?

Were the whole realm of nature mine,
That were an offering far too small;
Love so amazing, so divine,
Demands my life, my soul, my all.[32]

Notes

1 J. Jeremias writes: 'according to contemporary
   analogies Jesus must have intended that the Our
   Father should conclude with a doxology, but would
   have left the user to fill it in for himself' (quoted
   in Leon Morris, *The Gospel according to Matthew*,
   Leicester, IVP, 1992, p. 149).
2 e.g. 1 Chr. 29:11; Neh. 9:5; Ps. 145:21.
3 'The day Thou gavest, Lord, is ended', John Ellerton
   (1826–93).
4 Matt. 25:34.
5 Matt. 13:43.
6 Isa. 46:9–10.
7 1 Cor. 1:20–9.
8 Rom. 8:10; 2 Tim. 4:20.
9 Acts 7:55, 59. Cf. 2 Tim. 4:6; Heb. 7:16; Eph. 1:21;
   2 Tim. 4:8.
10 Dan. 12:2.
11 1 Cor. 15:20. Cf. vv. 50–7; Phil. 3:21.
12 Eph. 3:20, 21.
13 'O worship the Lord in the beauty of holiness', John
   Samuel Benley Monsell (1811–75).
14 e.g. Ezek. 1:25–2:1.
15 Exod. 33:18–23; 34:5–7; Isa. 6:1, 5.
16 Isa. 42:8; 48:11.
17 Mark 2:10; John 5: 22, 23; 20:28; 2 Cor. 13:14; Phil.
   2:9–11. Cf. Isa. 45:23; Rev. 5:13.
18 Extract from the Creed of Nicea, AD 325.
19 John 16:14, 15; 17:1, 5.
20 Acts 9:3–5; 26:13; 1 Cor. 2:8.
21 John 17:24; Rom. 8:18; Phil. 3:21; Col. 1:12.
22 1 Thess. 2:12.

23 1 Cor. 13:13.

24 John Stott quoted in Russell Chandler, *Understanding the New Age*, Irving, Texas, Word Books, 1988.

25 Rom. 9:5; 11:36; Eph. 4:6.

26 E. Hoffmann in *The New International Dictionary of New Testament Theology*, vol. 2, Exeter, Paternoster Press, 1976, p. 239.

27 Saul Bellow, *Herzog*, quoted in Millard J. Ericksen, *Christian Theology*, Grand Rapids, Michigan, Baker Book House, 1986, p. 1065.

28 Mal. 3:6; Heb. 13:8.

29 J. I. Packer and Thomas Howard, *Christianity: the true humanism*, Waco, Texas, Word Publishing, 1985, p. 95.

30 Thomas Goodwin (1600–1680), *The Work of the Holy Ghost in our Salvation*, Edinburgh, James Nichol, 1863 reprint, p. 144.

31 Col. 1:12, 13; Jude 24.

32 'When I survey the wondrous cross', Isaac Watts (1674–1748).

Also by Peter Lewis

The Colony of Christ
Hodder & Stoughton

'. . . this marvellous book' Alec Motyer

'Here is a most unusual book – a theological treatment of the doctrine of Christ which is both scholarly and readable!' Gerald Bray in the *Church of England Newspaper*

'This is a theology which has been preached . . . it warms and informs, lifting heart and mind to the grandeur of Christ, and humanity's place within God's purposes for this world.' David Atkinson in the *Church Times*

'An evangelical pastor's "Summa christologica" which is a powerful indication of both the humanity and divinity of Jesus Christ.' *Catholic Herald*

'The crying need of late 20th Century Christians is to recover for today the foundational place of Scripture and the centrality and all-sufficiency of the Lord Jesus Christ. Whether in the study of the pastor-preacher or as a handbook for all who would be clued-up Christians, or for home group leaders and their groups, both these needs are gloriously fulfilled.' Alec Motyer in *Evangelicals Now*

'A book that is destined to become a modern classic and a recognised authority for years to come.' Colin Whittaker in *Redemption*

505 pages   ISBN 0340 56894 1